WOMEN
NEGOTIATING
AT WORK AND AT HOME

FORLAGET SØERNE // SOERNE PUBLISHING

MALENE RIX

WOMEN
NEGOTIATING
AT WORK AND AT HOME

WOMEN NEGOTIATING
- At work and at home

Publisher: Forlaget Søerne, Copenhagen, Denmark
Print: Books on Demand GmbH, Norderstedt, Germany

Copyright Malene Rix & Gyldendal 2009 (Danish version)
English version: Copyright Malene Rix 2011, 2. edition 2019

Cover photo: Elisabeth Dahlberg / www.elisabethdahlberg.com
Cover design: www.workofheart.com
ISBN 978-87-996592-1-0

SUMMARY OF CONTENTS

Foreword   5

Chapter 1: What is negotiation?   15

Chapter 2: Process as key to a good result   31

Chapter 3: Gender as filter   43

Chapter 4: Negotiations in the workplace   61
Phase 1 – Negotiating with yourself   66
Phase 2 – Preparation and influencing others   74
Phase 3 – Striking the deal   88
Phase 4 – After the meeting   101
The Parallel negotiation   104

Chapter 5: Negotiations at home   113
Phase 1 – What do you want?   117
Phase 2 – Who needs influencing?   124
Phase 3 – How would you like your agreement to look?   127
Phase 4 – The aftermath – How did what you agreed upon work?   137
The Parallel negotiation   139

Chapter 6: Negotiators of the future   147

Appendixes   153

Recommended literature   161

FOREWORD

When you realise, once and for all, how often we as human beings negotiate, you will see it everywhere. I saw the light many years ago, when I participated in a negotiation technique course and discovered how useful a tool negotiation is. If you discover that you disagree with someone, it is quite natural for most of us to present arguments to support our own point of view and to try to convince the other person that you are right and that they need to rethink their position. I came to realise on this course how much more sense it makes instead to find out how to move forward together in spite of, and with respect for, the fact that we do not always agree. It was a revelation to me that something as dry and boring as negotiation could become an exciting and profitable alternative to endless discussion and power plays. It was a relief to discover that I could get what I wanted without necessarily having to fight with someone else, for one of us to win, the other lose. Luckily, I also discovered that you can work with negotiation both as advisor and trainer. It has been my privilege to explore the many interesting facets of negotiation throughout the last 10 years in close collaboration with great colleagues, particularly Søren Viemose to whom I owe a great deal.

My work in the field of negotiation
For many years I lived and worked abroad. I negotiated continually in both my work and private life, although I was not aware of it myself. At a certain point I worked as a producer and co-ordinator at Arken – Museum of Modern Art in Copenhagen. I took part in establishing and running the museum in its first, hectic years. Working in this environment made me realise, once and for all, how necessary it was to be able to create agreement between many and often quite different parties with opposing interests without ending up with serious conflict or high drama. I chose to do a course on negotiation technique and was subsequently offered a job with the consultancy company running the course. This became the beginning of my career as a negotiation advisor and trainer and by 2001 I had started out as an independent consultant.

I have since then worked with a wide range and variety of clients from both within the private and public sector. As an advisor and trainer in this field I focus on helping clients become better negotiators. During a training session participants are helped to discover their own experience and skills as negotiators, and at the same time they are given advice and inspiration as to how to adjust where necessary. Through exercises and feedback it becomes quite clear what works and when reactions and behaviour will not bring the parties any closer to an agreement. As advisor I get involved, for example, when two owners of a company want to part ways and have to agree on how to divide the company assets. In such a case I would help the two negotiators keep an eye on the future and how they move forward in the best possible way instead of trying to establish who did what, and why, and how would that translate into a reasonable selling price. In other words I help them focus their energy on finding the best possible deal for both of them instead of trying to find out who is right and who is wrong. I will encourage them to listen to each other's demands and the interests underlying those demands. I will ask them to find ideas and possible solutions to making a deal and to make sure that both of them feel they are getting something out of the agreement. My focus will be on *how they negotiate* – the process itself – and *how they communicate* as opposed to exclusively looking at *what* – the actual content - while working towards a deal.

Valuable experience from work and private life
Everyone negotiates on a daily basis. We all make innumerable deals, small and large, at work but also at home with the people with whom we share our daily lives. This means that we all have a great deal of experience as negotiators and that in fact most people are seasoned negotiators. This expertise that I claim we all have is not always used consciously or strategically. Few people are aware that they possess these skills and that they do in fact negotiate all the time. To realise how big a chunk of our daily lives we spend negotiating agreements with others is a great eye opener for many of the participants in my training courses. The realisation that we all do it and do it well can help pave the way for

using these tools more strategically in order that both we and the people we meet get more out of this process. The word 'negotiation' itself can seem both formal and inappropriate for some of the interactions we have, especially perhaps with our family and loved ones. However, the importance is not necessarily in the use of the word itself, but rather in the ability to be able to discover the possibility for negotiating in a conscious way in many more situations than we already do. It is for this reason that this book is also about how you use the techniques in your private life. Research in the area clearly shows that our negotiations at home have a great impact on the negotiations made at work, particularly the negotiation between partners, about career and job opportunities. Lack of equality in sharing domestic responsibilities, for example, will affect a person's understanding of how far she might progress in her career because she will consider if she can fit everything in, both her responsibilities at home and moving forward in her career (Becker 1985; Hersch and Stratton 1994). This is why it is particularly important for women to look at the negotiations they take part in at home, because the result of those affect our working life so much. One way to both have your cake and eat it, is to approach this challenge first and foremost as a negotiation with yourself: How can I combine all my wishes and wants for the best possible fit? This negotiation will then need to involve the people you live with, the people you work with, and perhaps it even needs to be taken to an organisational level. How can the workplace accomodate the employees' needs and wishes in both arenas - the workplace and the home?

Both management and staff
At the workplace management are often very conscious of using negotiation as a method in their day-to-day work, but employees also have lots of valuable experience from less formal and obvious but just as valid negotiations. Advice on negotiation in the workplace is relevant to both sides of the table. I include, therefore, examples from both management and staff perspectives. Furthermore, it would be relevant and rewarding to train both leaders and their staff together in how to negotiate in a con-

structive way. The focus of this training is not to learn tricks in order to get the better of your counterpart, but rather to find and use appropriate and helpful ways of communicating and leading the process to ensure that both parties get as much out of the negotiation as possible. To be able to spot ways in which you can get what you want without necessarily having to fight bitterly for it appeals to many modern professionals. The advice given in this book is relevant to all kinds of people regardless of gender, age, ethnicity or profession.

The constructive approach
To many people the word negotiation sounds a bit formal. They often relate this process to words like competition and struggle – a process that leaves some as winners and some as losers. Perhaps they view negotiation as a battle of words and arguments or simply that the person with the most power will also be the person winning the negotiation, even if it means forcing the result. When we discover how much we already negotiate we also realise how undramatic and perhaps even fun and fruitful this process can be. It is not arguments and pressure that secure a good deal. It is a constructive process where both parties are heard, recognised as valid partners and where their interests are considered: a balanced deal made in a good and respectful environment. Finding out how to plan and execute a constructive negotiation process is at the core of this book, as is the invitation to try out the recommendations at home and in the workplace. Our negotiations are also deeply affected by the filters we perceive each other through. One such filter may be about age. "She is an experienced woman, so I might not be able to fool her!" It may be about culture. "I'm going to negotiate a deal with this guy from the Middle East, so I'll need to think in terms of bargaining and holding on to my own demands as I'm sure he's great at getting a good price." It might even be about profession. "She is a free-lancer, so I'm sure she's keen to get the work. I reckon I can get her to reduce her demands quite a bit." These filters are also negotiated, but this often takes place parallel to the actual negotiation and a lot of it will be subconscious. In fact, in my perspective, we negotiate all the relationships we are a part of and

the way we relate to, communicate with and interact with the people surrounding us. This is why I do not think we can necessarily categorise people as being of a certain type - a static personae that is constant through life and in relationships. Rather, I think we have many different 'selves'. Certain aspects of our personalities are brought forward by the many and varied relationships we are part of in our lives. "How confusing," one could think! It is quite comforting for a lot of people to know what type they are, to be able to explain things with : Well, that's just the way I am! But on the other hand to be free of a fixed label – 'she's the introverted type' – can open up a range of possibilities to influence the story about you and what you bring into a relationship. You can negotiate and thereby partly decide for yourself what you want others to see and perceive of you – you can negotiate the story of you.

Men and women's terms in the negotiation process
If it is true that we negotiate our identity in many different situations, it becomes all the more important to discover and utilise negotiation as a simple but effective and in fact quite gentle way to navigate in a world full of relationships and choice. An important aspect of these 'identity negotiations' are the terms that exist for us as men and women in this arena. How can we use negotiation to change or improve these terms in the situations where they hamper more than help? When I teach women-only groups the only difference in content from mixed groups will be the focus on the terms we as women negotiate under. The advice and recommendations are universal, but they must be seen in the context of the advantages and disadvantages gender can impose on the process. A classic example of this is the proven fact that most of us expect women to be more conscious of and therefore mindful of others, or the group. This becomes significant when a woman asks for more than her colleagues in a salary negotiation. She might, therefore, seem more selfish than her male colleague, whom we expect to focus to a greater extent on his own salary and less on the group. This perception of the female negotiator can produce comments and arguments like: "Well, if you're to have that much more, what about the others?" This reaction to a demand for a raise may make the woman

feel guilty and make her reduce her demands too much or too quickly. Or perhaps the mere thought of being confronted with her 'greed' will prevent her from even asking for a raise, as she may have convinced herself, in her preparatory considerations, that it's no use even asking.

The structure of the book and its chapters
The book consists of three parts: looking at negotiation as a general phenomenon; what works when you negotiate; and how to work at home with the recommendations and the range of exercises referred to throughout the book.

What is it all about? – When do we actually negotiate and what terms and mechanisms does the process encompass?

What works? – How do you structure using negotiation both at work and at home in order to get what you want?

How do I practice? – How can I structure my thoughts about negotiation and the planning of negotiations?

WHAT IS IT ALL ABOUT?

Chapter 1 – What is negotiation will look at how to define negotiation. The purpose is to start the journey of discovery by finding out what we actually mean when we talk about negotiation, when it occurs and who it involves. When you look at the basic elements of all negotiations it becomes quite clear that it's a form of communication we all use, consciously or not. To know *when* you in fact negotiate is a fundamental condition to use negotiation effectively as a strategic and constructive tool.

Chapter 2 – The process as key to a good result will look into how utterly important it is to work on the process itself in negotiation, as opposed to focusing on content alone. The concern with content – the *what*

- is often at the fore-front of negotiators' minds: the money involved, the terms of the contract, the house or the car or even who does the dishes, which makes it easy to neglect the *how*. In contrast, the world of negotiation research and training is all about *the process* and how to develop and share thoughts, experiences and tools to improve the way we work when we negotiate. The reason for this consistent choice of angle is the fact that we as human beings interpret the result of our negotiations through the lens that the process becomes. An unsatisfactory, perhaps even unpleasant process, will make us dissatisfied with a result even should it happen to be a very lucrative deal objectively speaking. And vice versa, a good and fair process will make us happy with results that may not be the most spectacular. Interpreting each other and thereby *framing* the negotiation is a very big and important theme, so we will pay a lot of attention to all the filters that might affect the process.

Chapter 3 – Gender as filter delves into the very specific and pronounced role gender plays in negotiation. We can't avoid being perceived to some degree through our gender and this perception will affect the way we negotiate with each other. This filter will colour to a significant extent our expectations of the way we behave. It thereby creates different terms and conditions which men and women act under in this very special arena that is negotiation. In order to adjust these terms, if they are perceived as restricting, it is necessary to know they are there, which is why we look into this particular filter in depth.

WHAT WORKS?

Chapter 4 – Negotiations in the workplace is organised in four parts, each of which will look at a particular phase in the negotiation process. A central point here is the fact that negotiation does not just take place at a meeting, at a specific time, but stretches far beyond this to involve possibilities to work through both before and after the actual formal negotiation. It all starts with one's own thoughts about the negotiation where focus will be on what one wants and what to ask for. This first phase can be termed the negotiation with oneself. Then it's time to start influencing the counterparts, which is the second phase. Thirdly the actual meeting that takes place, where the parties will face each other and strike the deal. The fourth phase is the time after reaching agreement, where much work can still be done to secure its' afterlife and the continued building of the relationship. An underground current running throughout the whole process and all of the phases - *the parallel negotiation* - is the subtext of all that goes on above board and the place where the many aspects of our relationships are negotiated.

Chapter 5 – Negotiations at home will also structure the recommendations in terms of the four phases and the parallel negotiation. A lot of the advice in this chapter will to a large degree be similar to the recommendations from the previous chapter, although certain aspects will become more obvious and relevant to talk about here. An example is how the feelings that always abound in negotiations affect the process and how they are closer to the surface when we have to work with our nearest and dearest. This is why we will look into how strong emotions affect us and how we can use them as important pointers that help us in the right direction.

Chapter 6 – Negotiators of the future will round off the book by looking at how we all can prepare the ground for new generations of negotiators. If some of the terms we negotiate under – specifically those connected to gender – are negative or restricting, then it is up to all of us to change those. A good place to start is thinking about how we can create fair and equal terms for all negotiators regardless of age, gender, culture or creed.

HOW DO I PRACTICE?

The third part of the book is devoted to the various appendixes. There are exercises to work through and questionnaires to answer. These help you to work with and navigate the recommendations for the different phases.

All chapters are summarised by a series of questions that help translate the advice to one's specific and individual negotiations.

CHAPTER 1

WHAT IS NEGOTIATION?

WHAT IS NEGOTIATION?

Most people do not think about the fact that they negotiate all the time - but they do, we all do. The fundamentals of all negotiations are as follows:

> When two or more parties with different wishes, needs and interests who need to reach an agreement will go through a process with the purpose of reaching a result

This may sound a bit dry, but let us test this definition on a couple of situations from a seemingly 'negotiation free' life:

The colleague
Over coffee you and your colleague talk about an exciting project you have spent a long time preparing and to which your colleague has also recently been assigned. The time has come to delegate the project leadership, and you have an informal chat about this and other issues such as the need for someone to take on the role of coordinator and assistant to the project manager. As you get up to return to your desk and the work at hand your colleague says: "Well then, sounds great. So... I'll take on the project manager role, as I have so much other direct business with our boss, in fact I have a meeting with her just now. If you can then be the coordinator, which I know you're really good at, then it's all sorted. So let's just say that, then, eh?" And before you have time to react she has disappeared down the hall heading for your boss's office.

The partner
You hurry home from work in order to get the shopping done before you pick up your youngest child from nursery. It's not that late, so you manage both to cook dinner and help the older children with their homework before you all gather around the din-

ner-table. After everyone has cleared up, you look forward to an hour or so by the computer in order to catch up on all the things you left outstanding at work when you rushed home early. Out of the corner of your eye you notice that your partner has packed his sportsbag and is looking for his car keys. "Where are you going?" you ask, as you see your evening swamped by childrens' baths and bedtime stories. "Well, you went and did your aerobics the other night so I reckoned it was my turn tonight?" And with a smile and a wink, he's out the door.

The friend
The weekend approaches after a busy week, and you look forward to a couple of quiet days with no definite plans. Late on Thursday night your old friend from university is on the phone, a friend you have horribly neglected the last year or so which you feel very guilty about. He tells you how he will be in town this weekend with his wife and kids, and that this would be a great opportunity to catch up – especially since he's hoping they can all stay at your place? He goes on and starts organising how they'll bring their own sleepingbags, so if you'll be responsible for shopping food you can all share the cooking? You don't really get a chance to say no and this your friend takes as a yes. "Great! See you Friday and we'll only stay 'till Sunday midday. Can't wait!"

What happened here? How much say did you have in these important decisions? Are you happy with the outcome?

In all three situations there are different wishes and interests at stake, and these must somehow be resolved and agreed upon in order to proceed forwards. In the situation with the colleague two rather different roles in a project need distributing. With the partner, children need bathing and looking after, but the parents also need time for themselves. In the last example with the friend two valuable days-off are to be filled, or not so, as it may be, and a decision about how to spend them needs to be made. But in each of the examples given these decisions are made by others and come as a surprise or simply sneak up on you. The problem is that you miss the opportunity to influence properly a decision that will have an impact on your life. This is a shame really because a decision will generally be better - more robust and satisfactory for the involved parties - if everyone gets a chance to put their mark on the deal. So, to put it quite simply one can say: "When someone asks you for something, you have the possibility to negotiate. You can say 'Yes, if ...."

The definition
In order to be able to use all the advice and tools on negotiation it is crucial that you recognise this type of occasion when you see it! You might say that step one in becoming an even sharper negotiator is becoming aware of and being able to spot the negotiations that come your way. This has to be the starting point when you seek to have things your way. Step Two is developing a keen eye for potential negotiations, and this is when things get really interesting; when can you initiate a negotiation?

Let's begin by looking at the elements you'll find in all negotiations:

- **Two or more parties ...**
  In all negotiation we have interested parties. There will have to be at least two, but often there will be more, both actual and 'silent', i.e. not present at the table but with an interest in the outcome of the negotiation. Keep an eye out for situations where the interested parties are within your own head, as we actually quite often 'negotiate with ourselves', that is we have two or more conflicting voices having a discussion of pros and cons as part of reaching a decision about something.

- **with different wishes, needs and interests ...**
  If you agree from the start there is no need to negotiate. So when you start a negotiation it is because there is a difference - a disagreement – large or small. It is central to negotiation that

the involved parties have different wishes and wants: disagreement can give rise to a range of reactions and impulses in most negotiators.

➤ who need to reach an agreement ...

To disagree is not exclusive to negotiation, you can have differences of opinion in many situations. However, as soon as you need each other in order to move on and reach a result – an agreement – then the process turns into a negotiation. For example, a political discussion does not necessarily entail that the parties agree, it can simply be a straightforward exchange of opinions. The moment you need to decide whose opinion will count though, then the communication turns into a negotiation.

➤ will go through a process ...

Central to most negotiations are the conflicting emotions concerning a wish to reach an agreement quickly and painlessly on the one hand, and on the other hand the disappointment in many negotiations when the result is reached too quickly and you feel cheated of ... something? The process – *how we reach the agreement* – is the lens through which we interpret the actual result. So even if the result objectively speaking is great, the process also needs to be as we expect it to be, or we will devalue the agreement. So, you become a great negotiator by making a special effort to make the *process constructive* and reaching an agreement that all parties feel happy about. In this way you will make sure that both the objective deal and the lens that it is viewed through will make it a good result.

➤ with the purpose of reaching a result ...

The result, the deal or the agreement, the final decision or the contract signed – all these are goals that drive the process forward. The wish for and need to reach a result is there right from the beginning. If you do not agree from the outset, well then you negotiate, simple as that. You could even say that once you get a 'No' to some request of yours, it's time to negotiate!

➤ **which all parties are content with**
This is where 'negotiation' becomes 'constructive negotiation.' You could call it 'win-win negotiations' or Interest Based Bargaining (IBB) – all of which are terms that refer to the effort the negotiators using this method put into finding out what deal would ensure that all the involved parties get as much as possible out of the negotiation. By looking at the interests behind the demands you find much more scope and inspiration for creating an agreement that will reflect everyone's wishes to the largest possible degree. By choosing to focus on the interests behind the demands and trying to find ways in which all parties will get something out of the deal, you also automatically start working in a much more constructive way by asking more questions, thinking up ideas and suggestions and thereby making the process – the lens – much more positive and constructive than it would have been had the negotiators fought bitterly to maximise their own benefits with no regard for their counterpart's wishes and wants.

Now we have the basic framework of all negotiation in place, but just as seductively simple this definition is, so too, just as varied and manifold are the actual negotiations that take place in our lives. Negotiations can be about everything from climate control to higher wages for certain groups, from peace in the Middle East to better working conditions at your present job. From 'who does what' at home to when must a teenager be home on a Friday night? And then there is the most important negotiations of all. The basic negotiations you have with yourself about: What do I want?

Negotiating with oneself
It is absolutely crucial to know where you want to go with a particular process, what you hope to achieve by it, and why this is the right result

to work towards for you. This is both the backbone and compass in all the many negotiations you take part in. To get your bearings and find the 'lighthouse' which you navigate by in any negotiation, you will have to weigh the different options and make a decision before you start negotiating with others. This process can actually be one of the hardest, because this is where a lot of 'silent partners' can participate with very loud voices in the shape of society's expectations of you or those of the people that surround you. Considerations of other people's needs and wants, particular traditions or strong views on how one ought to behave etc. might clamour for attention and demand a seat at your negotiating table.

// RESEARCH ON... TO KNOW WHAT YOU WANT

When you start thinking about what you want, you can become a victim of what some psychologists call 'impact bias'. This happens when we convince ourselves that the effect of a given result will be bigger than what it actually turns out to be. Will the management title make you happy? The cottage by the sea? Two nights a week on your own? The discrepancy between what we persuade ourselves will be the effect of the outcome and what we actually get can be so large that we have a case of what researchers call 'miswanting'. That we often simply just don't know what we want and therefore accidentally wish for the 'wrong' things.

[N.Y. Times Magazine, September 2003]

If you stay up-to-date with what you fundamentally want for yourself, you will be a much stronger and more robust negotiator. At the same time, being clear about where you would like to go can give room for flexibility on the route to that goal. If you are clear about your own wishes and the interests behind those demands, then it becomes easier to focus the conversation not on *if* you get it but *how* you get it and inviting your counterpart to influence the route to the desired result.

Much of the advice on negotiation refers to situations you can plan and prepare and thereby be strategic about. Often, as we have seen earlier, a negotiation will arise spontanously or you find out about it *after* it is over. How to deal with these situations? One very important recommendation is that you regularly stop and think about what you want for yourself: what is important to you, both at work and at home? What are your core values and how would you like to live them out? What are your limits for how far you will go in trying to reach your goals? Or what are you prepared to do for others, and when is enough enough? If you think about these things on a regular basis you will have the foundations for a solid lighthouse to steer by in both planned and spontaneous negotiations, which will make them easier to deal with.

To find out what you really want may sound simple, but this is not always the case. Getting help in finding out what matters to you can be vital to ensure that all stones are turned and the issues are looked at from many different angles. A friend, colleague or partner can ask relevant questions and challenge your answers, and even a professional coach can be very valuable as someone to guide you in this 'conversation with yourself'.

A word of warning!
When we negotiate we often do this as a preparation to a negotiation with someone else. The interesting thing here is that in this situation there is a risk that you will concede and give admissions to the other party by reducing your own demands, i.e. lowering your first bid before you even start negotiating with the other. This can be wise, if you realise that your bid is so out of proportion to what the deal can hold, that an adjustment is necessary. However, it means that you will initiate the process with a lower first bid, which will affect the entire process. An internal dialogue where this is the issue sounds like this:

> "I really do think that it is my turn to get an increase in budget for my department, so I can hire the three profiles I so desperately need. But yesterday, at the management seminar, I heard that

finances are extremely tight at the moment, and I don't think any of the other heads of department will get an increase either. I suppose it is possible to deliver what we promised with the present budget, and if I ask for more right now it may be seen as being financially irresponsible, and there is no doubt my boss will get really irritated by my demand. Perhaps I should just lie low and wait and be happy that I won't have to let anyone go?"

Much research shows, that there is a clear correlation between how ambitious you are with your opening demand at the beginning of a negotiation and the level at which the negotiation ends. An important ground rule is: The higher your first bid is, the higher your end result will be. So be careful when negotiating with yourself not to reduce your demands too much in your preparations. One of the things that make us tone down our ambition is a worry that our counterpart will think that we are too 'greedy' if we start to negotiate at that higher level. Most of us want to keep a good relationship with the other party and therefore we consider the impact our demands will have on them. This affects our negotiations since we may reduce our first bid in order to avoid too much disagreement. When confronted by this fact most people defend their tactic by calling the more modest bid the 'realistic' option. But aiming for a 'realistic' bid is often simply disguising our fear of confrontation and being judged as a greedy person.

The parallel negotiation – the undercurrent in all negotiation

As if we didn't have enough to worry about with the infinite list of possible negotiations within which to navigate, we also have to deal with several layers of communication when we negotiate. When we try to reach an agreement, sit at a table and forge a deal, what goes on here is often just the tip of the iceberg: What and how much can each of us get out of this deal? But underneath the surface lies the bulk of the iceberg and what goes on 'beneath the table' greatly influences the actual deal. Apart from the specific content of an agreement many other things are negotiated simultanously. For example:

Power: Who is the more powerful person here?
Status: Where do we fit into the hierarchy respectively?
Influence: Who listens to who and how does my network compare to yours?
Sympathy and antipathy: Do I like this person? Or is there a lack of 'chemistry'?
Impact: Can she deliver on her promises?
Trustworthiness: Can I trust this person?

These things are not necessarily very concrete or even at the forefront of one's mind. They are negotiated unconsciously or hidden as a shadow or parallel negotiation. We all carry frames of references within us that we use when trying to decide if the person we're communicating with is worth listening to, is cleverer than us, good to have in our network etc. These frames of reference also contain ideas about how, for instance, a certain physical apperance or specific age group usually behaves or ought to behave. With these references we set out to adjust our relationship when we communicate with others, and this becomes particularly interesting when the purpose of our collaboration is to reach agreement.

In their book *Everyday Negotiation* Deborah Kolb and Judith Williams explain this level of the negotiation:

> "Negotiations, as it turns out, are not purely rational exercises in the pursuit of self-interest or the development of creative trades. They are more akin to conversations that are carried out simultanenously on two levels [...] All the time they are bargaining over issues, they are conducting a parallel negotiation in which they work out the terms of their relationship and their expectations."

As well as focusing on the actual issues of the negotiation, we also need to pay attention to this parallel negotiation which so greatly influences the results of the process. One example of the importance of this aspect is a story I heard from a woman participating in one of my workshops. This example shows very clearly how a particular set of references affect a negotiation:

> This particular woman is chair of a committee that donates money to various arts projects. She is in her mid-fifties, quite relaxed but also neat in her appearance with her hair up and discreet clothing. A meeting had been scheduled where two younger men were invited to present their application for a substantial grant from the committee. The chairwoman arrived well before the meeting was due to start and sat down in a corner of the room to prepare. As she sits there, the two young men arrive. They barely acknowledge her presence but sit down at the meeting room table and start talking about their strategy: What will we ask for first? How much will we be content with? And the whole negotiation is talked through. Our chairwoman hears everything. As the other members of the committee arrive, the woman rises and takes her seat at the head of the table stretching a hand across to welcome the two men introducing herself as chair of the committee.

In this parallel negotiation a range of unconscious frames of reference are at play, influencing how the two young men interpret the situation. Here sits a woman, middle-aged and discreetly working away in a corner and the men most probably think she is a secretary or at least judge her to be a person of no or little consequence. The dramatic 'renegotiation' of this particular woman's status, power and influence takes place within the space of the 15 seconds it takes for the chairwoman to introduce herself as the person holding the funding for their project in her hands. What the two young men see, when they notice a woman sitting quietly working in a corner before the meeting has even started, obviously does not harmonise with how they expect the chair of a committee to behave. So here both gender, age and appearance played an important part in the initial 'negotiation of the relationship'. In chapters 4 and 5 we will take a closer look at what to look out for in the parallel negotiation, and how you can work strategically with this level of the process to make sure it helps rather than hinders the actual negotiation.

We negotiate our identities

Negotiating our identity is in fact a constant process. Everytime we are with other people, there will be a measuring up of how we affect each other. Reinhard Stelter from the University of Copenhagen has identified the process by which we continually negotiate our identity (my translation):

> "Identity cannot be understood as something a person has as a stable and determined entity or fundament, but it is a process in which the person is permanently challenged to negotiate or renegotiate herself (or her self) in the various and changing communities or situations which the person will be part of (at work, at home, in her spare time, within the family). Identity does not have a fixed and inflexible goal, but is created via the person's staging of herself in various social constellations[…]where she will enter negotiations through the way she acts, through language and interpretation of social codes, and through the way she puts herself forward. At the same time the development of identity is affected by the person's ability to self-reflect and her knowledge about how others affect her and she them."
>
> (Reinhard Stelter: *Team – development and learning*)

Stelter sees our lives as one continuous negotiation with the world around us - about who we are in the many and varied contexts we are part of. To some people it might feel nice and reassuring to get a personality test and thereby get proof of, or an explanation why they are the way they are. But I agree with Stelter that we both develop our 'selves' and thereby our identities over time. I also agree with Stelter that we will be different people according to whom we interact with, and what the particular situation and circumstances are at a given point in time. This is why it does not make sense to me to look for a 'truth' about who we are. This can also limit us in our thinking about what it is possible to achieve. "I'm an introvert person, so there is no point in me even trying to be the life and soul of the party". When you start to pay attention to how we shape the story about ourselves through the way we act, speak and socialise with others, then we can work strategically and constructively with this parallel negotiation to ensure that it supports our efforts to get what we want for ourselves and others. We can have an impact on this negotiation about how others should perceive us. It will affect the story about you as a person if you always volunteer to do the boring jobs; or if you are engaged and active at meetings; or if you simply sit slumped passively in a chair for the duration of the meeting and rush out the door as soon as it is over. Do you behave in an ethically acceptable way, or is there a mismatch between what you say you believe in and what you actually do? Or, on a different note; Do you have a reputation for being a chameleon, who changes opinions to suit the environment? These behaviours - signals if you like - will colour the filters through which people see you: filters which may make an actual negotiation run more smoothly or grind to a halt.

If you consider the above in a purely theoretical negotiation context, researchers have looked into how our own perceptions or presumptions about how we 'are' will affect our behaviour in an actual negotiation. If we get too fixed an idea about how we are as negotiators, for example; "I am a tough but fair negotiator" – then we run the risk of not noticing the changing terms of the dynamics of the negotiation process and thereby fail to adjust our behaviour accordingly. This again means that we might get less of our interests and demands met, than if we were able to choose, from negotiation to negotiation, how to perform. If 'tough but fair' is not working in a given situation, then it can be helpful to have other 'identities' to work with, so we can meet our counterpart with an appropriate and constructive behaviour and communication style.

Discover and expand your possibilities for negotiation

Let's rewind a bit, to the time leading up to the actual negotiation. A very important point about negotiation is that it is a method: a way of working that can help you achieve what you want, be it a great bargain, a change, or an improvement! Some negotiations just come rolling along, but there are also many opportunities to seek them out, take an initiative and test whether this will be a helpful tool to get what you want. Here's an example of this approach from real life:

> A man enters a discount foodchain shop, grabs one of the shopping baskets and heads for the fruit and veg department. He fills his basket with a selection of things and then finds one of the sales assistants, who's in the middle of restocking the shelves. He asks: "How much for everything in the basket?"

Is this possible? Are you allowed to do this? Good question, which can only be answered by trying it out. The man in the shop got a discount, and the point here is: *he asked*. In Appendix I you can work on a personal overview of all the negotiations you might now discover you are a part of and become more aware of what you actually gain from these.

★ RECOMMENDED EXERCISES

Discover the negotiations you take part in, both large and small. Fine-comb your time at work, at home, and in your spare time for situations that are actually negotiations. Try to get an idea of how often you reach satisfactory results.

Keep an eye out for the parallel negotiations - where you are in the process of signalling who you are, what you can do and where you want to go. What do you actually do here? What do the people you communicate with do to position themselves and negotiate their identity?

Consider if you can initiate negotiations and thereby get something you otherwise wouldn't have.

Remember: When somebody asks you for something, you have an opportunity to negotiate. Say: "Yes, I'll do that if ..." and you have taken the first step towards a balanced agreement.

CHAPTER 2

PROCESS AS THE KEY TO A GOOD RESULT

PROCESS AS THE KEY TO A GOOD RESULT

When talking about negotiation it is often thought of as what happens from the moment we realise we need to negotiate with someone in order to move forward, through to the moment the agreement is reached. Sometimes this happens spontaneously and is over within the space of a few minutes. At other times, the process will continue for months, perhaps years even. Many negotiations continue, however, after they have been concluded, this being the case when the counterparts are people that we often negotiate with such as associates, colleagues and bosses and especially the people we live with. So our negotiations line up like pearls on a string.

The result is viewed in the light of the process
No matter how slow or how fast the process is, research shows that when we participate in a negotiation, we will judge the success of the outcome in the light of how good or bad the process itself has been. An example:

> You have been unhappy about your wages for the longest time because you feel they far from match the many assignments you have and the amount of responsibility you shoulder - especially when rescuing other people's chaotic and floundering projects. You actually do the job of two people since your closest colleague quit six months ago and hasn't been replaced. Your boss agrees to a negotiation about your wages, and you spend many hours systematically listing 17 great arguments for why you should get paid more. This includes documentation and lots of examples. At the beginning of the meeting your boss argues against your demand and says no to your request. But because you are so intent on convincing her of the relevance of your demand, you soldier on and stack many and elaborate arguments on her. Slowly your boss falls silent and leaves you to do the talking. You can tell she is tired and as time goes by the atmosphere grows very tense. In

> the end she gets up and looks at you, annoyed and folding her arms and says:"I'm so fed up hearing those same old arguments again and again, you're telling me things I already know. Can't you think of something else to say? You will get your raise, but know this, that the extra money you get will be taken out of the budget for all your wages, so somebody else will have to go without!" So you get your payrise but leave the meeting with a lump in your stomach and a bad taste in your mouth, and the good feeling of having achieved something just never really materialises.

In this negotiation the employee ends up with an objectively satisfactory result: she gets the raise she asked for, but the process was not particularly good – the route to the good result was not very constructive. So even if she gets an actual good deal, the joy of having achieved this is overshadowed by the tense atmosphere of the conversation. What if the situation were to develop a little differently:

> You meet with your boss to discuss your wages. She starts by asking you straight out what you want. You start by explaining the background for your claim. But your boss stops you and asks you to simply state what it is you want, in numbers. A little hesitantly you put forward your suggestion. "All right, that's fine, let's just agree on that," says your boss and reaches out a hand to shake on it with a broad smile on her face. A couple of minutes later you're outside her office, and one would think you would be cheering (soundlessly) but instead you walk down the corridor thinking, "Oh no, this was wayyyy too easy. I should have asked for more!"

A much more positive and markedly quicker process with a very good result, or what? Even when you get what you want without resistance, without long and draining discussions and bitter comments, then still you're not happy. Again, the *process* is key to the satisfaction with the result or rather: what is *expected* of the process. In this case, getting your way too easily leave you with the interpretation that you could have gotten more, because there was no resistance. If the expectations we have of the process are not met, then we interpret the result in the light of this surprise or disappointment.

Expectations of a negotiation result
Consciously or unconsciously most of us have certain expectations of the negotiations we face. If you notice the choice of words many people use when they talk about negotiation, you get an impression of what to expect:

>"I have some great arguments I can demolish my counterpart's claims with."
>
>"We'll just keep probing untill we catch them saying something that isn't true, and then we strike!"
>
>"If we don't speak right from the beginning, then we can lure them out of the bushes and reveal their tactics."
>
>"We're about to meet some really tough guys, but we'll stay firm – they won't get us down, and we'll fight 'till the last drop"
>
>"I'm aiming to win this one"

Many people describe their negotiations with words from the world of war or competition. On the other hand, it has also become quite commonplace to talk about win-win negotiations, because everyone sort of knows they ought to think this the best way forward. But it does not take a lot of scratching of the surface to discover, that most people view negotiation as a game or even a fight. The rhetoric surrounding negotiation will shape the expectations of what is going to happen. You're going in to fight for something. It will probably be rough. But, you self-righteously argue, you need to get them to give you at least *some* sort of concession. In this wording there is a very clear perception that negotiation can be conflict ridden because it is seen as a fight between opposing parties to distribute a fixed content. Expecting this will affect both how you *prepare for* the meeting and also how you *behave in* the meeting itself, and there is a risk that you will be negatively influenced by this. For example anticipating disagreement or opposition from your counterpart may make you think and act defensively, before you even meet. Not many people stop to consider *how* they will negotiate, but stay focused on content and what they wish to achieve. So, the point is, that *if* the process becomes the lens through which we view and interpret the result, then it makes a lot of sense preparing the *how* to negotiate. When we expect resistance and sharp competition, then most of us have a tendency to prepare razor sharp arguments and perhaps even threats."If he won't agree to this and sign, then I'll be sure to let him know what the consequences will be!" Also, there is a risk that you'll spend a lot of time thinking about how to 'expose' the counterpart and make them lose face, in the hope that this will make them cave-in and concede. On the other hand, if you view negotiation as an opportunity for the involved parties to gain more by working together than they would alone, then the groundwork is laid that makes it possible to approach the process in a more constructive way. To enter the negotiation with a wish to 'expand the pie' before you divide it, will urge the parties to investigate each others' interests, produce ideas as to how an agreement can accomodate as many of both parties' demands as possible and, only then, move on to the actual sharing of the pie.

From arguments to attentiveness
On many of my courses the participants show up wanting to "learn how to argue my case better, so I won't lose my negotiations" or "to find out what to do when the other person has better arguments than me." These requests mirror the common view that it is the *content* which moves the negotiation forward. This is why a classic way to prepare for a negotiation will be to stock up on arguments backed up by many data and long lists of examples or 'proof'. You could call it ammunition, which you aim to fire at the counterpart in the vain hope that some of it will hit a weak spot and magically open the drawbridge,- so that your counterpart will lean back in his chair and say: "Aaaah, *now* I see clearly. Of course you get what you want as you are absolutely right, I'm wrong and I'll immediately forget all my objections!" The idea that whoever is the better orator will win the negotiation is very

widespread. In reality it is much more about *how* you use words and *when*, than it is about clever arguments or the words themselves. In trying to get the negotiation started by using arguments and trying to convince the other party they're wrong, these efforts actually tend to work completely counter productively. A steady bombardment with lots of arguments will most likely result in the other person holding on to his own views for dear life and even becoming a bit stroppy as he tries to stem the pressure by applying a counterpressure. This ends up becoming a test of strength where everyone is holding on simply for the sake of not giving in.

Arguments and explanations are often used to convince a person or persuade them to do something. Arguments are designed for the purpose of making whoever listens as clever or enlightened as the speaker herself, and even making them leave their own standpoint and take on your views. In negotiation you need arguments, no doubt about it. If you want something from somebody, then you must be able to explain why. The interesting thing, however, is how many arguments you file away in your briefcase to take with you, how you present them and in what way you incorporate them in the work you need to do to reach an agreement. Instead of entering a negotiation armed to the teeth with 23 great (and some not so great) arguments, then just bring the ones that actually, clearly and most importantly support your claim. But then you'll run out of arguments pretty quickly, one might object. That's right, which is why the clear recommendation is to follow up on the presentation of your demand (what you want) and the 2-3 best arguments (why you want it) with a range of questions (how can I get you to give me what I want?). It could sound like this:

Demand:
"I want the corner office"
"I do not want to share it with anyone"

Arguments:
"'My job requires peace and quiet to have conversations with important clients on the phone"
"I need space and privacy to have meetings with these clients."

Question:
"What do you think about this?"

Perhaps you get a 'yes', but even if you get a 'no', then you continue asking *questions*, which will serve to investigate the 'no' instead of *arguments* designed to persuade the other to agree with you:

More questions:
"What will it take for me to get that office?"
"Are there other offices that might meet with my requirements?"
"When will an office like this become available?"
"Can we discuss other ways of meeting my needs?"

Now the conversation gets going because the person sitting opposite you is not blown away by a flood of arguments and explanations that they will need to defend themselves against - if they can't just say yes. Perhaps they won't be able to answer the questions up front either, but then you take a break and let the ideas and suggestions of the questions have some time to work.

Both content and process
You can say that negotiations always consist of content and process. By focusing on making the process and the way you work with the content as constructive as possible for all parties involved, then you make sure that the content gets the best possible chance of developing into an agreement both full and fair enough for all. By working with process as the key to a good negotiation you also minimise the risk that exists of making the classic mistake of conceding on your own demands in order to get the process rolling and making angry people happy again. You

don't actually need to give your counterpart a lot of things to make them happy. All you need to do is ensure that the process towards a result is satisfactory for everybody. To give in and concede on some of your demands is something you need to do towards the end of the negotiation process where the actual bargaining takes place, and even then you only give something, if you get something else in return.

// RESEARCH ON... WHAT MAKES A PROCESS FAIR?

When researchers look into what it takes for people to feel that a negotiation is fair, they look at fairness in terms of both distribution of content and the process itself. It turns out, that if you perceive the process as having been fair you will interpret the result as fair as well, even if the objective distribution of content is not. Also, the negotiators who feel that they have had a fair process are more likely to adhere to the actual agreement. On a general level it has surprised researchers to find how limited the effect of an objectively fair distribution of content is as compared to the effect achieved when negotiators feel they have been part of a fair process. Summing up the research in this field in the words of Professor of Law Nancy A Welsh:

> "Perhaps what is most interesting about the research that has been done regarding fairness perceptions is the extent to which it undermines the iconic image of two rational stranger-negotiators locked in a battle of logic, economics, and will. Rather, the research reveals that negotiators' aspirations and moves will be significantly influenced by the culture and context within which they are negotiating, their own self-interest, and most intriguing of all, their social connection to each other. Ironically, as negotiations become increasingly global and virtual, it may be the development of old-fashioned relationships that will be found to matter most of all."
>
> [Nancy A. Welsh: Perceptions on Fairness]

So, if you wish to make your negotiations as good as possible for both you and your counterparts, then you need to work specifically on the process itself. If you develop some good habits of working contructively with the negotiation process, then you can use these tools and methods in all your negotiations, be they at work or at home. Appendix II contains a range of questions which will help you evaluate your (successful) negotiations and discover the good habits you already have, but perhaps haven't discovered yet.

Process as 'The Great Filter'
The fact that we interpret negotiation results and evaluate each other through the experience of the process makes it into a 'filter' - but it is a many layered filter. It is very easy to just say: "All you have to do is make the process a good one" but what is a good and contructive process when you negotiate? Where to find and install something like that? And how do I actually do it? The word 'process' contains a lot of elements. A good process can be all about respectful and appreciative communication. It can be about sitting in comfortable chairs enjoying a cup of coffee made especially for the meeting, or simply having enough time and a calm environment in which to explore properly the parties' wishes and wants and all the inherent interests. Not least, a good process can be about sending and receiving unspoken or even unconscious signals to each other every time you meet. This is why negotiators often talk about 'framing' – illustrating how we all look and perceive the world from a subjective and deeply personal perspective that is coloured by our life experiences. Our personal histories and the circumstances we live in become part of this 'Great Filter', which helps us make *a* reality *our* reality.

Every one of us carry around many and complex ideas about how the world is or ought to be. Some time ago a newspaper published a picture of the new Minister of Defence in Spain. The picture was not a middle aged man in a suit, but a young, pregnant woman who was inspecting the troops that were lined up, wearing a flowery maternity dress. When you look at this picture and read the caption a whole range of frames or filters that many of us carry internally are slightly disrupted, as we might have expected something else.

Part of the frame we adopt when negotiating has to do with all the things we see and hear and therefore use to judge or 'compartmentalise' our counterparts: their age, where they live, their physical appearance, level of education, tone of voice and accent etc. And then there is our gender. A lot of research has shown that gender is a major factor when we try to place the people we meet and negotiate with, and make up our minds on what to think of them and the possible outcome we can achieve. The next chapter looks at this single, but very important, factor in the 'filtering' process and how it affects the possibilities we have as men and women in a negotiation.

✶ RECOMMENDED EXERCISES

Try to discover how the process in a negotiation affects you and the person you negotiate with.
Notice and make a note of what works well in a given process:
- The way you communicated
- How you listened to each other
- If and when you recognised and gave credit to each others' demands and interests
- Gave each other room to work with the content to produce a good agreement

Look at your own 'filters' – have you placed the people you negotiate with in certain prefabricated frames? How do these frames affect the way you percieve your counterpart? Are they helpful or not?

CHAPTER 3

GENDER AS FILTER

GENDER AS FILTER

When people talk about gender and negotiation it often ends up becoming yet another slightly depressing statement of the fact that also in this area, women are lagging behind. "Women are not very good negotiators" is a comment I hear surprisingly often - also very much from the women themselves. A clear proof, often given, is the difference in wages between men and women – still a fact in a range of areas of employment in many countries. It is for this reason that I will begin this chapter by looking into why this perception of women's negotiation abilities is so widespread. I will start from some, perhaps rather glum, facts about the terms women negotiate under; the circumstances surrounding negotiations in which women take part. This is where the biggest differences lie buried. When a woman asks for a payrise, it simply sounds different from when her male colleague does the same. She will more often and a lot quicker be perceived as 'too greedy' than her male counterpart would. This is a major factor, which to a large degree affects our chances of success when we negotiate. Women have to work harder and for longer than men to achieve... less! We simply meet more resistance when we negotiate. After looking into this aspect of how gender affects negotiation, I will turn to more optimistic thoughts. Basically you could say that women are at least as proficient negotiators as men – but a lot of women haven't noticed this about themselves, and consequently they do not put this skill at the top of their list of what they think they are good at. This widespread perception about women's negotiation abilities will affect our expectations when we sit down to do a deal with a woman. The great news is, that there is absolutely nothing wrong with women, their genes or biological make-up. The differences in how we negotiate and the results we achieve lie primarily in the terms we are allotted to negotiate under, and these you *can* negotiate! Women negotiate all kinds of things all the time, as do we all, so there is huge experience to draw on, and great potential for becoming an even better and, most importantly, a more conscious and strategic negotiator.

Gender as filter and how it affects the terms of the process

When discussing the filters of negotiation – filters which colour the way we perceive each other and how we behave – it is especially interesting to discover what role gender plays. Gender is a very important aspect when talking about negotiation, because perceptions of gender are inextricably linked to thoughts of power and status, and how to determine who actually decides what in a given situation. This is significant in a process designed specifically to deal with distributing resources etc. Some classic comments I have heard many, many times from the women I teach are:

> "Negotiation is both fun and exciting if and when I do so on behalf of others, but when I have to go and negotiate something for myself, I tend to get a mental block and all of a sudden it becomes very difficult."

> "It is very easy for me to be both very straightforward and persistent in my demands when I negotiate everything else but my salary. When I'm about to ask for a payrise, I turn into this apologising and embarrassed person, and all my selfconfidence goes out the window."

Interestingly enough many women think themselves very good negotiators *in certain situations*. When you start looking into these successes, it turns out that these women almost automatically have adopted a style of negotiation, which gets them very satisfactory results. But the element of negotiation that concerns *wanting something* - demanding more than you already have - comes out most clearly, when the demand you make is for something personal. All of a sudden, the strategies you use in all other situations look and seem less acceptable, because you are fighting on behalf of yourself, and this is unfortunately no longer considered a 'good cause'.

The root of this change of perception lies, as I have already mentioned, in traditions, cultural practices and prejudices we carry around that colour the way we interpret other people's behaviour and thus will 'allow' some people to ask for and others not. This is where a lot of research unfortunately shows that we all, often unconsciously, expect women to be generally more modest than men, and therefore less likely to make ambitious demands on their own behalf.

// RESEARCH ON... BEING AMBITIOUS OR JUST PLAIN GREEDY?

Linda Babcock and Hannah Riley Bowles from the Carnegie Mellon University in Pittsburgh, two of the foremost researchers in the field, have recently found that women, who are ambitious on their own behalf, are 'punished' by those they negotiate with. If a woman asks for and insists on, getting more than the proffered pay at a job interview, she is deemed less attractive as a possible new employee/colleague than a man making the exact same demands with a background that matched precisely. And it was both men and women, who deemed that the 'greedy' woman would not be as nice to work with as the man.

Most of us have a relatively accurate sense of what the world expects of us, and this will influence the way we act. This is one of the reasons why women generally, as it turns out, ask for way too little in negotiations. If we are met with greater resistance than our male colleagues, then perhaps we chip away at our demands before we go to negotiate in order to avoid hearing, or perceiving an echo of 'I think you're being a bit greedy here', when our counterpart says no to our demand.

Differences in circumstances matter
We are now at the heart of understanding how gender affects negotiation. In their book *Women Don't Ask* Linda Babcock and Sarah Laschever explain, that the act of asking for something, be it a payrise, more interesting work projects or greater authority etc., is something

many women struggle with particularly *when negotiating on behalf of themselves*. The book describes the results of a wide range of tests and research that show how big a challenge it can be, for strong, independent and extremely competent and experienced women, to be ambitious enough on their own behalf. This has prompted the two authors to write a follow-up with the meaningful title *Ask For It,* where the training programme they include in the book very much focuses on practising asking for something you are likely to get a no to! The more often you ask for something and get a no, the more robust and courageous you will become with regards to testing the boundaries of the negotiations, in which you take part. There is a reason why you as woman might have a tendency to become more cautious when negotiating - all the more reason to try and change some of the standard perceptions and expectations that produce this behaviour. There are obviously many more opportunities for women today than in the past. But this cultural change has perhaps been faster than the adjustment of the perceptions that we have inherited from the past, of gender appropriate behaviour concerning distribution of labour at work and at home. The traditional division of the jobs to be done at home and at work have benefited some groups more than others, which may make them reluctant to change the state of affairs. An increase in equal opportunities has meant that there is a much sharper competition for the same jobs, careers, self-development possibilities etc. and thereby new discussions emerge about the fair distribution of *all* jobs, including the less exciting tasks that are part of our daily lives (read: making the coffee, writing up the minutes for the meeting, doing the laundry, washing the windows etc.).

Negotiation is all about distributing something. To even start a negotiation, there will have to be some demands, someone has to ask for something, saying: "I would like." Then there has to be someone responding to this demand by saying: "Well no, you won't get this just like that." If you simply get a yes, there is no need to negotiate. That men and women negotiate on different terms is all about what we expect and assume about the behaviour of the different genders in situations, where we ask for something for others or ourselves; when we say no to somebody's demands; or if we only agree to give something, if we get something in return. A woman participant on a course told me the following story:

> The person concerned was a young woman with a good job in the public sector. Her salary was not quite as high as it should be for someone in her position, and at the annual salary negotiation she asked for more. Her male superior rejected her demand, but she kept at it and even made suggestions as to how she could get what she wanted in ways other than just by raising her salary with x amount of money. After several, and sometimes lengthy, negotiations, her boss conceded and gave her a raise. A couple of days later she met him in the hallway, and her boss gave her a wry smile and said: "Hey there, here comes the greedy girl." Of course the woman was shocked at first, and then she was quite upset to know, that this was the label she had gotten just by asking for a raise and working persistently to get it.

Lionesses or Bully Broads?
This example is from the real world. It is quite recent and here we are not talking about an ultraconservative and old fashioned company, but about a contemporary public sector environment. In a negotiation you have to be able to formulate your demands. You need to be both persistent and robust when working towards achieving this – but it is sometimes easier said than done. If you perceive or experience what this woman did, of course you will be affected by it. It was quite obviously not as legitimate to ask for something for herself, than had she fought for a bigger budget for her department 'like a lioness for her cubs.' This aspect is reflected in many of the comments I have heard in the many years I have taught negotiation technique. A survey of a group of women evaluating how they perceive themselves as negotiators identified a number of perceptions. "I am really good at negotiating deals with clients/ ressources for my department/ conditions for a project, but when I have to negotiate my own salary, I get stuck and feel incompetent."

But is it not the same process, identical tools and useful habits that you can use in most kinds of negotiations? Well, yes, and then again. The very important difference here is, that in asking for something for oneself, there might be a clash, conscious but often unconscious, with our perception of how women behave or ought to behave.

Some negotiation literature recommends that you toughen up, take a deep breath and insist on your rights with selfrighteous indignation in your voice and perhaps even demonstrate a 'male' type of stubbornness, arms crossed and lips clamped shut. At the other end of the spectrum we find training programmes for women, who are deemed unacceptably masculine by their surroundings, and who must 'relearn' to be more feminine as quickly as possible. These women are called 'bully broads' and they have committed the sin of behaving like men: to be quite clear and unapologetic about their own ambitions, to have a conversational style that is direct and without frills, to look people squarely in the eyes and not show emotions readily or demonstrate weakness. This type of behaviour is not of course in itself wrong, but by some it is perceived as too harsh and provoking by others, so these women are sent on courses where they learn to modify their expressions, show a degree of uncertainty about their ideas or competences, to hesitate when talking, to avoid too much and too direct eye contact! These women are asked to change by those who interpret this as 'bullying' behaviour, although objectively speaking they simply act the way we expect *men* to.

It is always a good idea to watch other negotiators and notice what works for them. But to simply adopt, uncritically, a traditional 'male' negotiation style, will probably backfire. And why change behaviour completely *if an adjustment is all it takes*? It is not a question of cultivating the feminine or the masculine when you negotiate, but rather to find your own style of negotiating based on what you already do that works, and watching how others get results. Both men and women are good negotiators, when their negotiation is based on an honest intention of reaching a result that will work for the parties involved, including themselves. The possibilities for securing this balance is just not the same for women as it is for men. It has to do with the circumstances that follow from the tendency we all have to categorise people according to gender. But how to change circumstances that, at first sight, benefits men more than women?

Securing equal circumstances have positive consequences

I asked Kenneth Reinicke, gender researcher at the University of Roskilde, how he thinks we can improve equal opportunities between men and women? One of his clear recommendations was, that we work on making it very clear 'what is in it' for those who must relinquish a privileged position. Instead of giving somebody a bad conscience, or blaming and accusing those with privileges, then the whole discussion about equal opportunity should much rather focus on what everybody will gain from correcting the imbalances there may be. It must be made clear what enormous advantages you gain from creating equal opportunities, both at work and at home. The recommendation must be very clear, that you negotiate your way to a fair balance instead of trying to argue your way to more equality. If women see men as resources, perhaps particularly at home, then the seed is planted to optimise seriously the sharing of all the available ressources in a collaborative way. You can do this, for example, by mapping out all the parties' wishes and wants, as well as their potential, when you negotiate your way to more equality. A redistribution of tasks and responsibilities requires that you take the time to identify what you yourself would like to contribute, and what the other person wants to chip in with, and then work on dividing the total amount of tasks and responsibilities. A process like this can be both very sensitive and conflict laden as it most probably involves change, and particularly if the new division of labour challenges firmly rooted perceptions of, for example, gender patterns. Negotiation is a useful tool to help you navigate this process.

The small difference

Gender has always been a part of defining and creating a reality that looks different for men and women, and for better or worse. Naturally there are physical differences, but the perception of gender difference that play such an important part of our daily lives has to do with more than just these physiological differences. There are still researchers who claim, that most gender differences can be traced back to the Stone Age and our biological heritage. This perspective only goes a little way in explaining some of the more obvious inequalities, but it is tempting to explain it all away in this manner. This attitude is abundant in quite a lot of the literature you find in the field. One of the best known examples of this viewpoint is found in John Gray's *'Men are from Mars, Women are from Venus'*. One explanation of the popularity of books that describe in no uncertain terms how 'this is simply the way women and men *are*', could be the need for us as human beings to create some sort of order in the multitude of social relations in which we move both at work and at home. It is convenient to have some models explaning how things are, so there is no need to investigate further or question these differences and what effect they have on our lives.

In her book *The Myth of Mars and Venus – do men and women speak different languages?* the researcher Deborah Cameron has the following suggestion for why we love the 'myths' of men and women's differences, even if they are not based on scientific evidence:

> Though we often think of stereotyping as something only the ignorant and prejudiced do, the truth is that we all do it to some degree. ...(stereotypes)... are widespread because they fulfill a vital function in human societies. They are short cuts which help us to deal with new people and situations by reducing the complexity of human behaviour to manageable proportions. But of course, stereotyping has a downside: it can reinforce unjust prejudices, and make us prone to seeing only what we expect or want to see.
> [Deborah Cameron: *The Myth of Mars and Venus – do men and women speak different languages?*]

Deborah Cameron sets out in her book to dismantle the claims and so called 'truths' many of the books like *Men are from Mars, Women are from Venus* build on. Her starting point is a very central myth: that men and women communicate in different ways. There is an overwhelming amount of evidence that suggests, that we communicate in the same way much more than we differ (a linguist has calculated the overlap to be 99.75%). What is different is primarily the *positions,* from where we speak. The interesting thing about this thought is that we, both women and men, are not born to either rule the boardroom or manage a flock of kids, but rather that the difference lies in which arena we are invited *into*, and which we are excluded *from*. You could say, that it is not that we have inequal opportunities because we are different, but rather that we are different because we do not have equal opportunities. If gender is a social construction, then society has helped keep a focus on and strengthened the differences that have suited particular situations and times. An example could be the perception that women are more caring and 'soft' in their dealings with others, and therefore are better suited to certain professions. Instead of becoming irritated that we as women have been dealt the 'compassion gene', this insight can open up a range of possibilities to change and dismantle some of the inflexible myths and prejudices, that form part of the explanation why the genders are different. As the two professors of economy, Catherine Eckel and Philip J. Grossman, and Angela C.M. de Oliveira Ph.d note in The Negotiation Journal October 2008:

> "Though stereotyping (by both men and women) is still alive and well, it is often unfounded. As we as negotiators begin to recognize these subconscious biases that are brought to the bargaining table, we will be able to negotiate a better outcome for ourselves and the parties we represent. Men and women most often behave in similar manners. In the instances in which they behave differently, women behave in a manner that would help build long-term relationships and that would help teams reach agreements in delicate situations. Men, on the other hand, behave in a manner that would result in a better starting position but potentially hinder the ability of the negtiators to reach an agreement. This highlights the

importance of incorporating the "stereotypical strenghts" of both sexes into negotiation strategies."

Differences in gender and status
Associate Professor Karen Sjørup has undertaken extensive research and taught gender studies for many years at Roskilde University. In an interview she offered an example of what I would translate into a parallel negotiation of status and influence, where gender matters. She was talking about Italian researcher Silvia Gherardi's work on gender in organisations:

> "She talks about a notion she calls the ceremonial celebration of the difference in gender; that it's appropriate to give women compliments, that as a woman it is important to be good-looking, and that women should dare to be feminine. Silvia Gherardi talks about the 'repair work' that follows in the wake of these practices, namely in the situations where we as women crave recognition as indiviuals on the same level as, and with the symbolic accept of, us as 'one of the boys'. It is all about how to construct oneself as a gendered individual that a man should be attracted to, and the resulting double standard which might produce an uncertainty about one's professional merits.

So, not only do we negotiate from gender specific roles and positions, we are also busy negotiating our gender itself when we interact as men and women. This negotiation is difficult, or as Karen Sjørup says: "Like walking on the knife's edge" because for most people there are quite specific and therefore different things we are willing to expect from the two genders. There is a fine line between using a gender 'advantage', and when this very same advantage becomes a liability. It is important to note that the 'advantage' might not be perceived as such or even used this way by the person in question, but it may still be what others see. One example is the former Home Secretary in the UK Jacqui Smith, who caused a minor uproar when she addressed the Commons about terrorist attacks in London in July 2007 dressed in a quite formal suit but with a slightly low-cut top underneath. Asked about her reaction to the media attention on her dress, the Home Secretary replied: "Funnily enough, the main thing on my mind when I got up was not is my top too lowcut or not?" (Mailonline October 2007)

Another forum where there is a difference in how we perceive and hear men and women is on the strategic arena in an organisation - the meetings and situations where important decisions are made. To get involved in the political game or the strategic workings in the workplace seems to appeal far more to men than women. Karen Sjørup describes it like this:

> "I often find that women don't seek out the information which would enable them to act on a political and consequently a superior level of an organisation. This also applies to some men, but much more often to women. On this level it also becomes apparent how a statement, an attitude to something will get recognition in a group. It usually has to come from a powerful male in order to have an effect. If you get up and make a statement as a woman, no one will refer to this. If a man will say the same thing, then everyone will refer to what he said, and in this way women are marginalised in the game that this is. Here one needs to be really thick skinned in order to keep getting up on that podium and making a statement."

Karen Sjørup also talks about how many women today are obvious and very strong contenders to challenge the rule of the 'old male dinosaurs' that have dominated historically. Women are often better educated and less humble, but many may choose to avoid the political settings because they cannot be bothered with the conditions under which they get to operate. The influence it gives you to get involved at the political and strategic level in an organisation is not just something, which will have an effect on specific or concrete issues. It will also affect the negotiation itself, when it is decided who is worth listening to and putting your money on - all of which takes place in a parallel negotiation. This again will influence the actual negotiations taking place in the workplace and what expectations we have of individual negotiators and their ability to forge strong and important deals.

Conditions can be changed
So, the conditions we often negotiate under are far from perfect. Luckily, however, the obstacles women face in negotiation have everything to do with the possibilities we are given and the prejudices we are met with, and very little to do with our actual negotiation skills. The many, many negotiations, where women achieve fantastic results both on behalf of others and for themselves (both at work and at home), are proof that women are very clever and competent negotiators. There is a tendency to downplay these results, either because they are taken for granted or perhaps don't count for as much as the hardcore negotiation results of a substantial wage increase and high status, that some people secure for themselves. If women negotiators don't talk about and draw attention to their results, it will affect the parallel or strategic negotiation that takes place constantly where one's reputation as a negotiator is formed. If women negotiators to a larger degree discovered, accentuated and celebrated the results they achieve, then that in itself would be a step towards changing the rather common view, that women are not as competent negotiators as men. You need to take credit for what you achieve, perhaps even boast about it. Since some of the terms you negotiate under is determined by the fact that it sounds slightly less positive when women emphasize their results than when men do, then it becomes important to find ways to navigate around this obstacle and still be able to 'show off'. This could be for example to become so thick skinned, that a raised eyebrow and crossed arms won't deter one from making strategic demands on one's own behalf. Finding constructive but also strategic ways of influencing our negotiations without having to simply adopt a very direct and confrontational style of negotiating will do much to improve the conditions we work under.

Great negotiation skills

The way forward is much more about how to become a competent negotiator than how to fight against the possible negative factors of gender, age or ethnic background that may affect the process. Gender is a strong filter. It is the first thing we find out about someone, when we see them. Is that a woman or a man? It's hard to conceal your gender and the filter it constitutes. It will affect our expectations of a person, which again is marked by our prejudices. In fact, the most effective way of breaking down the barriers that prejudices about gender present in negotiation is by being... a great negotiator. Women are more than qualified to become even more constructive and effective negotiators because of the modern emphasis on the interest-based approach to negotiation. The expectations of how we as women ought to behave, and the conditions these traditional perceptions have given us in negotiations, have also no doubt helped women develop certain skills more than others, for example, to be generally thought of as good listeners. It is, therefore, not the point that women should learn to negotiate in either a self promoting masculine way or in discreet, feminine ways, but simply that we should all strive to negotiate like collaborative and self assured individuals. Some of the very core skills and abilities the modern successfull negotiator has are:

> **To be a good listener** and show interest in the person, you negotiate with
> **To have respect** for and be able to cope with viewpoints and wishes that are different from one's own
> **To be able to build good relations** and work to keep them healthy
> **To be creative** and innovative when it comes to finding solutions
> **To be able to focus on forging deals** instead of being proven right

Many women will be able to identify themselves with this picture of a great negotiator, which means that they are more likely than not already there! The opposition they have been confronted with in their negotiations has affected many women negatively, so they have perhaps become too modest in their demands in order to avoid being branded 'greedy' and being confronted with a resounding 'No!'. The negotiation in that event may be over quickly, but there's a great risk that the full potential of the negotiation has not been explored in the rush to get out of this potentially difficult situation as quickly as possible. But even if the negotiation process and the arena in which the negotiation is conducted has often been fraught with obstacles, particularly for women, this has not stopped them from developing a range of contructive methods, which allow them to make great deals and long lasting agreements. For example, one could speculate that because women historically have been expected not to speak at official gatherings or meetings that this factor may have been significant in developing skills that somehow would get around this fact. This could be part of the reason why women more often than men use a more facilitative style of communication: Asking questions and listening to the answer (the two don't always go together!). Inviting more people into the conversation instead of 'holding the floor'. And, the simple fact that women talk less than men do (thus allowing for more equal sharing of attention). This last fact may surprise many, as there is a very persistent and strong myth, that women talk more than men, but recent research has shown that men actually take up more 'speaking time' than women – both at work and at home! This may be a sad fact in some ways, as less time to speak equals less influence, even when we finally get a chance to talk. But if these conditions have made women develop a more appreciative communication style, this is a great advantage when looking at the skills demanded of a modern, collaborative and constructive negotiator. To be able to build and maintain good relations with others through the way one negotiates, is also a skill often attributed to women. This skill is perhaps also a result of women having to operate in negotiations in slightly hostile environments, where you as a 'demanding' woman meet more resistance, and therefore need all the friends you can get. Researchers have found that negotiators, who work purposefully on building a balanced relationship with their counterparts in negotiations, also achieve better and more robust results. However, being aware of the benefits of good relations can affect one's wish to stay in or rather; get out of, the sometimes conflict-prone process a negotiation may be. So, being socially intelligent is something worth cultivating, especially if one is also aware, that this can become an Achille's Heel if and when the concern for the relationship becomes more important than working towards one's own goals. The trick is to combine relational awareness with the knowledge that the relationship might be affected by the negotiation but being prepared for this. The dissonance that might arise from the initial disagreement -and all negotiations start with some kind of disagreement - is not likely to cause permanent damage to the relationship, especially if you choose a negotiation style which focuses on being tough on the problems to be solved but gentle with the people involved. Use Appendix III to investigate whether gender affects the conditions you negotiate under.

The longterm perspective
There is a general and ongoing negotiation of women and men's conditions for making good agreements which takes place every day, and which will shape the future for coming generations. Our perceptions of what women and men could or should do, are allowed to or dare to do, is something we can all influence and this obligates us to work for more equal opportunities for negotiating for women and men. One important arena for this is the personal relationships of which we are a part. Children watch and learn from adults, and if you have only ever seen your father pay for everything on family outings, then this will affect your perception of who is in charge of the money (and all the fun that comes with this job!)

I had a chat with a 10 year old girl while we were walking along a harbour front. She spotted an incredibly nice and expensive boat and she got very excited about how luxurious and fantastic it looked. "This is the kind of boat I would like to have when I grow up, so I better find myself a rich boyfriend!" This spontaneous outburst made an impression on me, but as we talked a bit more about the boat, we agreed that the cleverest thing to do in the long run was probably to make sure she became rich herself, so she could buy just the boat she wanted. Our little talk ended up by her starting to speculate about what it would be like to do business studies somewhere abroad when she grew up.

Women don't have to start doing all the plumbing at home or move heavy furniture around, if they don't want to. But what we signal to younger generations is significant: a lot of our perceptions of what is appropriate or even possible for women and men to do will be passed on down through the generations. That more fathers might take the biggest chunk of the allotted maternity leave or take 6 months off to be home with their small children, will send a forceful message that family life and careers can be organised in many different ways. That more women choose to become CEOs and become public figures consulted in the media on this background will likewise broaden our perception of what is both 'normal' and acceptable. And this is where we are lucky. We have the possibility to renegotiate the conditions for meaningful co-existence that we have inherited. We can take a stand on them and change them according to our needs.

✶ RECOMMENDED EXERCISES

In what situations are you aware of your gender? In the workplace, at home or out in society? What is it that makes you aware of your gender in these situations?
Are your possibilities for getting what you want affected by your own or others' perceptions of gender? Are there conditions you would like to change?
How do you or others work to counteract the potentially restricting conditions? In actual negotiations or in the parallel negotiations?
Which ideas about what women and men can and ought to do or not do, do you pass on to younger generations?

CHAPTER 4

NEGOTIATIONS IN THE WORKPLACE

NEGOTIATIONS IN THE WORKPLACE

In the first three chapters we have focused on finding out what negotiation really is and how many layers you can dive into and examine in order to become a little wiser about this unique process. This next part of the book will concentrate on 'what works', that is - advice and recommendations you can use in actual negotiations. The workplace is a very central arena for negotiations of all kinds, and it is the place most people associate with this way of working. So, let's look at all the big and small negotiations we're a part of there.

Wage negotiations
Two people apply for identical jobs. They have the exact same qualifications and experience and are both 30 years old. They both get an offer of 4600 Euros a month. One of them negotiates a higher starting salary and ends up getting 5000 Euros, the other accepts the initial proposal of 4600 Euros. If both get a yearly payrise of 5% of their current salary, how big will the difference in earnings be for these two, when they reach the age of 65?
The answer is: approx. 429.000 Euros, which is the accumulated earnings you get from negotiating for a higher salary ONCE!

Most people associate negotiation in the workplace with those we have (or don't have) about our wages; when we get the job and then on a yearly or regular basis. Many international studies of how we negotiate our wages conclude that men, more often than women, won't settle for the first offer they get from an employer. This is particulary marked when you look at how men and women behave differently during the whole process of negotiation and not just at the negotiating meeting itself. It is all about how you position yourself daily, how you draw attention to your worth and continuously influence the ones with whom you negotiate. The following story is real and a classic example of the many positive consequences that you can bring about, when you are being ambitious on your own behalf, including when you are talking about your wages:

An economics graduate is about to get a job in a large, financial institution. He is not the only one they hire. The company has taken in a whole 'batch' of graduates with the same degree. This is why the company has a standard rate for employees hired at this level. This young man, however, negotiates persistently and manages to get a slightly higher salary than all the rest (around 65 Euros more per month). This slightly higher outcome of his negotiations, apart from earning him a little more money each month, has the following effect: When management are looking over the budgets for staff, they will notice 'the guy that gets paid more than his peers'. He gets noticed because he obviously is a more valuable employee than the others, and he certainly knows how to negotiate! This makes him the natural choice when younger members of staff are handpicked for further training, development projects or management positions. You could say, that that extra bit of money jump-starts his career, and this particular young man did indeed rise quickly in the hierarchy of the company.

This example shows what you can achieve by demonstrating that you believe in your own worth. An important point here though is, that precisely this type of 'I'm-a-little-better-than-the-rest' tactic at a salary negotiation works better for men than for women. If a woman graduate insisted on the same it might have a more negative effect, as shown in the research conducted by Linda Babcock and Hannah Riley Bowles (described in chapter 3). But it doesn't detract from the fundamental thought that it might be worth raising a few eyebrows or facing some resistance, if the positive effects of this, rather short term, discomfort will have so many positive effects? Not to mention the fact that the more often women behave like this, the more 'normal' it will seem.

If you want something from somebody, you will have to be someone this person sees as relevant and interesting enough to make a deal with. Perhaps you already have a formal position which gives you the power and the mandate to negotiate, but that doesn't always mean you automatically have genuine impact. Your position can be supported though, as this story illustrates:

> A woman participant in one of my courses told me how she as a young, blonde and quite petite woman from the city had to negotiate an important deal with a delegation of older men from a rural area. In the first meeting she got the distinct feeling that they didn't take her seriously. It was never said out loud, but negotiations were clearly affected by this. At a certain point she simply ended the meeting, packed her bag with a remark about how she couldn't see them getting any further today, and traveled straight back to the city to the amazement of the gentlemen in the delegation, who hadn't expected a young woman like her to come all this way and leaving without an agreement. When she next came over to continue the negotiation, there was a clear improvement in the level of respect they showed her.

A central element in this story, is that this woman behaved in a way that strengthened her mandate (she broke off the meeting and took a time-out in stead of giving in to the pressure), and this is very important when building up bargaining power and impact. You need to demonstrate, on an everyday basis and on as many occasions as possible, that what you do, the results you produce, the person you actually are is both relevant and interesting to the people that hold the key to your negotiation results. If you clearly demonstrate that the person you negotiate with will achieve more by dealing with you than by not doing so, then you are well under way to positioning yourself and building up your power at the bargaining table.

Negotiating other things at work

Often when talking about negotiations at work focus will be on pay as the most obvious thing we make agreements about. However, all the mechanisms mentioned above also apply to a range of other things you can negotiate in the workplace:

Better assignments that will result in relevant experience and a good take-off for advancement

More responsibility which translates directly to higher wages as well as paving the way forward careerwise

Strategic posts on teams, committees etc. which will help position you

Training which can be both personally stimulating and developing key competencies

More flexibility which can help secure a better balance between work and private life

Travel expenses and paid participation in important events that make you visible, consolidating and expanding networks

Perhaps this is where you think: 'Well actually, I don't particularly care about all the material things. For me the important thing is to do a job I find meaningful and working with colleagues I like and value – this is a reward in itself. Why strive to climb up the career ladder, earn more money, become more visible and get more responsibility?' These are very relevant considerations which deserve to be taken seriously. In fact, they need to be taken so seriously that this is where you need to start: the thoughts you have about yourself as a working person and what you hope to achieve from your job. This is part of the work you need to do in the first phase of the negotiation: the one where you find out what you really want.

PHASE I – NEGOTIATING WITH YOURSELF

What needs changing or improving?

If you ask people if they have a job description most will answer yes. If you ask them if this description is complete and up-to-date, however, most people will say: "Oh no, no". A significant angle on what it is you actually do should include whether this is the most satisfying thing for you to be doing, and is it that which makes the best use of your abilities and experience, both considerations that are most relevant to your career and your job satisfaction. It is at this point that most people will hesitate and think long and hard before they answer. So therefore, it is in this scenario of considerations that you should actually start; by getting an overview over:

> **The present:** What do I actually do, and what do I think about it? What makes sense, and when am I wasting my time?
> **The future:** What would I like to do more of? How would a perfect future look for me jobwise?
> **The past:** What relevant education, training or experience do I have? What positive experiences at work can give me a hint as to what I would like to do in the future? What kind of work have I found meaningful in the past?

In order to think about all these things you need time and space and perhaps even help from someone, a partner, colleague, a close friend or even a coach, that will help you maintain focus and make sure that you dig deep into your motivations and examine closely your own thoughts. Appendix IV consists of a range of questions and tasks you can use to help you get an overview of what you wish for, and to make a plan for how to approach upcoming negotiations to get what you want.

As a general rule you can say that the moment you want to change something, to achieve something or get more of one thing or the other - this is a signal that it is time to negotiate. When you are asked to do something for somebody, this is also a chance to negotiate. Actually you could say that whenever you get a 'no' from somebody, when asking for something, then there is a possibility to start a negotiation. In order to benefit from the possibilities you have for changing and improving your own life and that of others, you will more often than not have to initiate this change. It is not enough to just sit and wait for an invitation. You need to get out there and ask for what you want. When you have spent time and paid attention to what you really want from your (working) life, then this will be a lighthouse to navigate by in the process you embark on. Perhaps your vision about the final result is a bit hazy. But this is fine as it will enable you to be open to other or better solutions and outcomes than you initially had pictured. The important thing is to establish where you would like to end up: less stressful working days, better pay, more respect, fewer routine jobs etc. etc. and then be open to ideas and suggestions as to how you get there.

The interests behind your demands
You could say that the core of what you demand must represent your interests as much as possible. Then you have shaped the foundation for what is called, in negotiation vocabulary, *interest based bargaining* (IBB), where the participants work towards satisfying the interests behind their demands rather than fight about who is right and who is wrong from locked positions. An example:

> You prepare yourself for what you would like to get out of your next salary negotiation. You are, in fact, quite fed up with most of your current tasks, but say to yourself that a payrise will probably help to compensate. Therefore your demand will be for more money, which will be the focus of your talk with your employer. But even if you do get some more money, it will not solve the basic problem of an unsatisfactory job content.
>
> Alternatively a proposal could be to be relieved of the most cumbersome of your tasks in exchange for taking on other, more relevant jobs – possibly in a different part of the organisation. As these new tasks would demand more of you, you will also need to be compensated with higher wages. This proposal could also contain suggestions and ideas for alternative paths for you onwards and upwards in the system; to your need for paid training; or simply ideas for how to map and talk about your worth as an employee, and how best to use your skills and abilities and how this can be reflected in your salary.

It is always a very good idea to examine the facts and do some serious benchmarking. This process provides inspiration and is an important input to all your thoughts about what you would like out of a negotiation and what you are worth. What do others get paid, and what is it they do to get this pay? How is your kind of work organised and rewarded in other organisations? What have others done to get to where they wanted to? When you know as much as possible about the content of your proposal and the facts it builds on - possibly with the help of friends, colleagues, union representatives, networks etc. - it will make it much easier to find alternatives and improvements when you meet resistance to your demands in the negotiation. To be prepared to find 'alternative routes' to the result you wish for will make both the agreement and the process towards it much better, than if you have only one thing on your list and it becomes a do or die situation for you to achieve it.

The ambitious proposal
Now we are getting close to the moment when you put pen to paper and your actual negotiation proposal, your demand so to speak, needs to be formulated. This is also the first time you tell your counterpart what it is you would like from this negotiation. So, you have been thinking, talking, examining the facts and researching for information and ideas as preparation for deciding what you want. And now it is clear to you: the honest but also realistic proposal for an agreement. It is neither too much nor too little but exactly what you figure to be realistic, so this will be what you ask for. Or not? In the previous chapters I described the importance and significance of the process itself in the interpretation of the actual negotiation result. A fundamental expectation of the involved parties in a negotiation is, that that when you negotiate there will be a movement – a change in positions - where each party will give a little untill you end up somewhere in the middle. If you start by asking for what you would be content with, also sometimes called your *'breaking point'* - what you think is fair and reasonable but which would also be the bid, where less than this would not make you happy - then you won't be able to give any concessions to your counterpart at all thus cheating

them of the 'movement' or concessions they were expecting. The breaking point is often called your BATNA; the Best Alternative To a Negotiated Agreement where less than this will make it irrelevant to negotiate and you will walk away. What you need to do is to make an ambitious proposal or first bid: a request that, when granted, would make you so happy and pleased with the negotiation that you would call your friends and family and boast about the outcome. A solution that you would think about with pleasure in your daily work and that would make you feel like doing an even better job. If you present an ambitious proposal, then you make it possible to give concessions to your counterpart without settling for less than your breaking point, and you might even end up with a better than just 'realistic' result. This is where some people have strong objections, especially when we're talking about salary negotiations. "This is like a Middle Eastern Bazaar! It's a silly game when both of us know that this is how it works, and that makes it ridiculous to even participate in!" For some people it is of the greatest importance to be trustworthy, to mean what you say and stick to it, and to them this strategy is interpreted as pure exaggeration, which would make them seem untruthful. From this perspective it would make most sense to ask for what you want, neither more nor less, which often turns out to be the 'breaking point'. But the result is that in order to *not* get less than your minimum request, you'll have to sit, arms crossed throughout the whole *process* and not be willing to move an inch. Not a particularly fun negotiation, and even if you use a long list of arguments like - "But this is just the realistic bid, I have already reduced my demands, so it is the least you can give. I have looked into the facts and they all point towards.....etc.etc." - then your counterpart will perceive you as hard and inflexible. Unless you cave-in under the pressure from the other party and end up with less than your minimum demand.

The optimistic, ambitious first bid at the beginning of the negotiation will not get rid of an initial 'no' to your proposal. But even here research shows, that a high bid will influence the person you negotiate with over time and will lift the bar for where the whole agreement could end up.

A comprehensive and ambitious demand will adjust the counterpart's perception of the level of the agreement upwards, and at the same time, it will give you the possibility of actually reducing your demand a bit along the way and give concessions, thereby creating the 'movement' we talked about earlier. And so you kill two birds with one stone.

// RESEARCH ON... AN OPTIMISTIC FIRST OFFER WILL PRODUCE BETTER RESULTS

It has been proven that a negotiator with optimistic wishes or aspirations will get better results than those who are less ambitious. This is primarily because an optimistic negotiator will present a higher first bid, which will define the range of the negotiation. Secondly, an optimistic bid will ensure that the negotiator making the bid will work harder to get it and, last but not least, it will make the negotiator more patient. As well as being optimistic in your demands, it is also very important to be precise, as this will ensure that you keep your eyes on the ball and counteract letting yourself be too swayed by the other party's bid or by the process itself. Instead of asking for 'a reasonable payrise' you need to state quite clearly what kind of payrise you expect, and this demand must be based on what you yourself believe in. You will come across as far more credible when you ask for something which is based on an optimistic as well as an ambitious wish than when fighting for something arbitrary which you have decided upon without much thought or preparation. It often becomes quite obvious in the way you communicate, whether you mean what you say or not. (Andrea Kupfer: Aspirations)

The optimistic bid is what one course participant once described as: 'That which you would feel slightly uncomfortable asking for.' The point here being, that if you yourself think that you're perhaps a little too ambitious, then you are probably avoiding the trap of being too modest. On the other hand, if you find yourself thinking: *'This* I can definitely ask for' – then there is a risk that you may have reduced your demands a bit too much. Asking for too little is often the result of trying to avoid a reaction to a demand that indicates that you have been too greedy, which is how a blank refusal might be interpreted. But think about how dissatisfied you would be if you simply got an 'Okay, that's a deal!' to your demand. It would leave you thinking that there must have been more where that came from. So, what we are aiming for, is to establish the first bid as one to which you are *sure* you will get a no! In this way you will find the boundaries for the negotiation, and then you can work towards a place where the parties can agree.

Think about how children negotiate and notice especially how they initiate the process:

>"Mum, can I please have the jumbo size chocolate bar, some chips and a large Coke?"
>"Absolutely not! What are you thinking?"
>"But can I then have that regular chocolate bar, some chips and a Coke? Please?"
>"No way. You won't be able to eat anything else – it's far too much"
>"So, can I have some chocolate and a Coke?"
>"Allright then, you can have a small chocolate bar and a small Coke, and then I don't want to hear another word, allright!"
>"Yesssss!"

It may be a trivial example, but what you often see when children negotiate is that their first bid is very ambitious indeed, even though they know full well that they won't get it all. By asking for a lot and slowly reducing their demands, they make sure to get maximum benefit from their negotiation. They are not particularly affected by the many no's that come at first. Consequently it becomes quite a natural thing to explore the negotiation boundaries every time. An independent journalist and communications expert I once interviewed was quite clear about how her asking fees were in fact an important part of positioning her in the top end of the spectrum of independent advisors. By asking for what advisors at the top of the game asked for, she sent an important signal that she had the selfconfidence to ask for a high fee, and she also indicated her level of professionalism. She knew that her asking price was too high for some, but she had thought long and hard about it and decided that she was prepared to lose jobs in the short run, because she was convinced she would gain in the long run by becoming known as a competent *and* expensive advisor. So, making an ambitious first bid comes at a price: you might get a resounding no. But no's you can work with. If you can't transform the no to a yes, then you will still leave the other party with the impression that you know your worth, and that you have the selfconfidence to ask for it as well *even* if they can't give you what you want at that point in time.

★ RECOMMENDED EXERCISES

Practice your ability to seek out and take advantage of the many possibilities there are for negotiating. Try initiating at least one extra negotiation a week. Keep turning up the volume once you have discovered how much you gain from simply *asking* for what you want.

Consider if there is anything you would like to change or improve:
- Work assignments, working hours or responsibilities?
- Salary and work conditions?
- Assistance/ delegation?
- Holiday/ time-off?
- Training?
- Participation in conferences/networks?
- Participation in strategic meetings or fora?
- Physical working environment?
- 'Extras': sports membership, book allowance, meals, computer, telephone or subscriptions?

Find out what you want and what these things would do to change and improve your daily (working) life. Get help from colleagues, partners, friends and family to discover your worth and avoid being too modest.

Let your first bid be ambitious: What would you really *really* like to get out of this negotiation? Find your breaking point: the least you are willing to accept. The range between your ambitious first bid and your breaking point will give you room to maneuver and give some concessions, or 'movement' in the process of negotiating.

Consider the positive effects your ambitious first proposal could have: What will it say about you as an employee? Who will be affected by this 'story about you' or what reputation will it give you with people and in situations other than the person with whom you are negotiating here and now?

PHASE 2 – PREPARATION AND INFLUENCING OTHERS

All your thoughts about your own wishes and wants have paid off and you now have a well thought through first bid lying on your desk. Sometimes it would be nice if it was then simply a question of going right up to the person you want something from and simply asking for it, getting it and going home. Most people hope, that once they present their demand things will magically move forward and a deal will be made. Instinctively most people also know that things probably won't go quite as smoothly as this. Such a premonition is often the cause of nervous flashes and sweaty hands before you enter the negotiation meeting, and, more seriously, may also make you defensive and overly rigid about your demands.

Arguments are not enough
Not a lot of negotiators simply give in, abandon all their own demands and give you what you want without batting an eyelid. They need to be

influenced by someone or something in order to see the point in giving you what you want. This is where you encounter one of the most common tactics in negotiation, which is trying to influence your counterpart and making them give you concessions by presenting them with arguments - lots of arguments. Unfortunately it turns out, that what makes negotiators 'move' and give concessions is rarely arguments, and never *just* arguments:

> "I would like to get funding to do this leadership training course, please."
> "I'm afraid we don't have the budget for that."
> "But I need some inspiration and some leadership tools, and a lot of my colleagues have been on the course."
> "Oh well then, now I understand, that sounds reasonable. Of course you can sign up for the course."

Not really. The arguments presented to support the demand for leadership training are fine and make sense, but they don't make the employer's budget any bigger. "Management should have thought about this when they planned their budgets" you might object. Yes! Exactly! If you want to influence the result of the negotiation you are about to embark on, you need to start well in advance of needing to reach an agreement. If your boss has been made aware of your needs on a regular basis and at the same time has been presented with the advantages of sending you on a training course, then she will have ammunition for *her* negotiation for a bigger budget for her department. This means that when you embark on this phase of the negotiation you need to work on the following:

Find out who has a say in this negotiation? Who makes the decision whether you get what you want?

What are the terms and conditions for your counterpart in this negotiation? Who do they negotiate with? What does their world look like?

How can you influence them, so they will want to give you what you want? What do they need to know in order to understand your demands? What new ideas and suggestions can you come up with that will make it easier for them to give concessions?

Influencing on a day-to-day basis

Making sure you are clear about your goals and get noticed on a daily basis, both by showing the results you create and letting others know your needs, will both influence and help the person you are going to negotiate with to navigate in this process and find ways to give you what you want. I often get strong protests from course participants who hear this as urging them to 'butter someone up' or manipulate your counterpart. To try and influence someone can seem like manipulation, but my recommendation is simply to make sure, that the person you are going to negotiate with is properly prepared to do so: That this person has all the relevant facts (which you have supplied); that they know what you do (which you have been kind enough to give them regular up-dates on); that the person knows what your wishes are (because you told them). We all influence and affect each other all the time, automatically and without thinking much about it on a daily basis. It will not make it a criminal act to think about and make some of this activity conscious and strategic by sowing the seeds you later wish to harvest, and doing so well in advance of rolling out the John Deere harvester. This makes sense because it turns out that we are all much more susceptible to being influenced with regards to an upcoming negotiation *before* and even *after* the official negotiation meeting itself. Here is an example I heard from a course participant:

> A partiular department in this organisation works in a large, open space office with the manager's office right next door. One of the employees had the habit of performing a wild dance - American Indian style – around a large green plant in the middle of the office, every time he had secured funding for one project or another. The rest of the department were sick and tired of this perfor-

mance, which was primarily meant for the manager's eyes and ears (his timing always coincided with the manager being present and his door open). When the time came for the annual salary negotiations this particular employee got the substantial raise he asked for with little effort. A coincidence? I think not.

Many of us wouldn't dream of loudly proclaiming our great results and beating our chests to drive the point home. Luckily other and perhaps less offensive ways of letting the right people know what you achieve can have the same effect. If you were to translate the 'victory dance' to a more palatable way of influencing your counterpart in negotiation, you might consider doing one or more of the suggestions presented in the overview of the phases before and after the actual meeting. The examples are based on a framework from a book by Danish negotiation expert Søren Viemose, and it shows what you can do to sow the seeds necessary in the periods leading up to the meeting. By doing this, you move up front some of the hard work of shifting your counterpart in your direction to times and venues other than the actual meeting. The actual meeting itself can in fact be quite unsuitable, because of the often strict timelimit and the way the parties are locked into positions on each side of the table. Most importantly, when your counterpart arrives at the meeting, he or she *already knows* who they want to give what to, and how they see the agreement being formulated. This position makes it very hard to persuade them to give substantial concessions. This is why influencing the people with whom you negotiate needs to be something you do on a regular basis, and well in advance of the meeting where a deal needs to be agreed on. There are many ways to do this important work, and it is up to you to choose the particular actions and processes which will make up the strategy that best suits you. You must decide when and where it will be both appropriate and viable for you to do this, but do it you must! Recommendations for how you handle the meeting itself, once it does actully happen follows in the next section.

Phases/Activities	Day-to-day	Before the meeting	The meeting	After the meeting
	Be visible and accessible and let your counterpart know about relevant results, thoughts and needs you may have	Look into and agree on what you each expect of the meeting		Appreciate the agreement and the fact that your counterpart has given concessions – say thanks!
	Make contact and initiate or keep up a running dialogue with your counterpart; show an interest in their world	Find out what your counterpart's interests and demands are, and make it clear what your wishes and demands are		Show your counterpart that what they gave you has had the desired effect and that you honour your part of the agreement
	Have informal meetings and seek out situations and arrangements your counterpart may be a part of in order to build a relationship and share information	Have informal meetings where you plan the process and exchange demands		Help your counterpart in showing their colleagues or superiors that they have made a good deal
	Think of the parallel negotiation and how you would like your reputation to be	Forward any relevant information that might be useful for your counterpart and which will support your claims		Evaluate the process and adjust to make it even more constructive
		Get help influencing your counterpart from others who might have an interest in the negotiation outcome		Continue the day-to-day influencing as preparation for the next meeting

Here is a true story that shows how influencing the people you negotiate with works both ways.

> A young woman had come to the conclusion that she deserved a payrise. She actually wanted a 10% rise and she started talking about this to her boss about 9 months before the annual negotiations were due to take place. She conveyed this message at several occasions throughout this period of time, but once the time of year came for the actual negotiations to start, management decided to disclose what they had in mind for this year's round of talks. The general message was, that they could give a maximum of 4% wage increase. 'Oh-oh' thought the woman but, unlike others, she kept repeating her demand. So, by the time her negotiation meeting took place, everyone involved already knew what everyone wanted. She asked for 10% and got 8.5%!

Management influenced the staff by letting everyone know the limits for the negotiation. By doing so, they wanted to make sure that the employees adjusted their demands accordingly. The woman influenced her boss by being clear about her expectations well in advance and *in spite of* the general message from management.

To influence someone you will have to use the tools at your disposal, and these will be subject to your actual situation and the possibilities it offers with regards to, for example, the level of access you have to the people you negotiate with, the means of communication you use etc. Since the advice is to work on your negotiation primarily before the meeting, then you must think about how to go about it. As a general rule you can say that because negotiation contains an element of disagreement (you ask for something you don't just get), then the best thing to do is to meet with the person you negotiate with in order to have as many channels of communication open as possible. Having said that, influencing someone happens on many different levels, and you can easily use both telephone and email to work on the important task of finding out who your counterpart is and what they are thinking, as well as planting the things you would like them to be affected by in this negotiation. You could, for example, agree with the key persons that need to notice your results, that you will send them an update by email on a regular basis in which you tell them of your results but also tell them about about your needs and wishes. This kind of email can be an alternative to the dance around the green plant from the previous story, and it is often much more do-able than rolling out the carpet for an 'I Did It My Way' performance in the office. In fact there are no holds barred with regards to ways of influencing people: a quick call to hear how things are going, an informal chat over a cup of coffee which, although it's informal, will be about the state of affairs in the organisation, an email with a link to a relevant article that supports your goals etc.

Getting noticed on your own terms
By being visible and showing your results in a way that suits your temperament and circumstances, you will also demonstrate that you are valuable to this organisation. If, in addition, you also make sure to indicate what it would take for you to keep working like this and being this committed, then you achieve two things. Firstly, that there is something to be gained by the person with whom you negotiate by them giving you what you want e.g., a payrise. And secondly, that there is something to be lost by this person if you no longer work there. This is not to say that you have to walk around dropping hints that are thinly veiled threats about how easy it is to find work elsewhere. Making threats in a negotiation will most likely create strong resentment on the other side of the table, and this will increase the risk of the process spiralling out and becoming more conflictual than it needs to be. Focus should be on what it will take for you to keep producing the good results that you have shown. Everything you say and do will obviously have an effect on the people you negotiate with, so attentiveness is necessary.

To take responsibility for the process and guide it so it becomes constructive is also part of building up your reputation as a negotiator, and it will affect the stories told about you in this connection. When we talk about how to influence your counterpart and what you yourself can do, I often get the comment: "I don't see the person I negotiate with on a daily basis and I don't run into them in the hallway either. So all this influencing on a regular basis, is not possible for me." Well, yes, you can still gain by influencing them, but it might take a bit of creative thinking and new ways of working. You might want to do some of the following things:

> **Consider** how information about you and your results, wishes and interests can reach the people that you need to influence. Can you; send the information? Create visibility around you and your cause via articles or other media? Arrange meetings or get-togethers in which your counterpart will find it relevant participating in?
>
> **Look up** these people over the phone, by email or suggest a meeting which could very well be about your upcoming negotiation. Even if the negotiation is not imminent, then think about how you can prepare the ground by establishing a good relationship with your counterpart and start influencing them, while it works.
>
> **Find out** who *does* have access to your counterpart even if you don't, and start influencing them. It's quite possible to influence someone via others, and generally this is about making sure that the right story about you is being told in the fora in which your negotiators participate. This is where the parallel negotiation becomes even more important. What is your reputation at work? What stories are told about you? And are they the right ones? Who is in, or ought to be in your network, who could become an 'ambassador' for you in the right places?

If you haven't even persuaded your counterpart to come to the negotiating table yet, then think of this as a 'negotiation about the negotiation' and use the advice on being clear about what you want ("I would like to make an agreement with you about improving my working conditions"), ask about when and how this could be possible ("When would be a good time to talk about this?") and not be too thrown by an initial 'no' ("What will it take for us to start working on an agreement about this? If not now, then when would you be prepared to talk about this? Can we start a conversation about this now and then wait and reach an agreement later?").

Email as a forum for negotiations

As electronic communication formats become the preferred and the easiest way for a lot of people to work and communicate with each other, it is inevitable that a lot of negotiations will take place partly, or completely, in this forum. There are both advantages and disadvantages in using email as negotiation tool:

Disadvantages:

Social distance: The email format has a certain in-built social distance. This makes it hard to communicate such that isn't fact because you miss the tone of voice, a face that sends endless messages by its expressions, and the 'sense' you get of a person by seeing them in person

Misinterpretations: If, regardless of the impersonal nature of email, you try to make it informal and social then it's even easier to be misunderstood, especially because we are more sensitive than normal when negotiating due to the fact that we are by nature adversaries (we don't want the same thing). So an ironic comment or a humorous response may be taken literally and have the opposite effect of what you intended

Arguments: To stick to the facts and be unable to focus on the relationship and the process will enhance the risk of the negotiators choosing to work primarily through arguments. As we have seen previously, this is not what moves a negotiation forwards. It will often be replied to by counterarguments and the process grinds to a halt

More parties involved: It is very easy and tempting to involve others in your negotiation by a simple click on the cc-button, especially if things get difficult. Unfortunately more parties in a negotiation will also make it harder to reach an agreement. More participants can hamper the process and increase the risk of interference from more or less constructive individuals, that may not themselves have any direct role in the negotiation but nevertheless feel the urge to get involved

History: Often email negotiations flow back and forth between parties by the 'reply to' function. In this way the whole 'history' of the negotiation is clear to all, and the parties are often reminded of how much they disagreed at the beginning and 'fall back' on old arguments and remember the, perhaps sharp, tone from the start of the process

Advantages:

Efficiency: The most obvious advantage for many is that it is a fast and effective way to communicate, especially when negotiating with someone to whom you have no physical access

Less focus on status: You may miss certain social indicators, but this can also be an advantage in certain situations where power and influence get to mean less, simply because there are fewer ways of demonstrating them. This is particularly significant in negotiations where there are imbalances or terms that favor one party over the other. An example could be the difference in perception referred to earlier when it comes to demands by ambitious women for higher wages by contrast to men. By cutting out the spontaneous reactions from the person with whom you negotiate, you can tone down the risk of caving in or giving up because the stern look and crossed arms you get as a reaction to your demands is invisible. It can give you that extra bit of support you need in order to make an ambitious first offer and ask for what you really want

Visibility: Email is a great medium for conveying important information and documents to those you need to influence. The weekly update on your activities might be easier to send than finding the time and the occasion to drop by the boss' office and tell them how things are going. The necessary 'self promotion' can be easier to work with by email than face-to-face

We can't disregard email as an integral part of many negotiations, but use it with the above comments in mind. Negotiation can be a very sensitive process and you need to put in both hard work, a lot of patience and persistence meanwhile ensuring you work in a constructive way for things to succeed. Therefore my clear advice is to use email by all means, but combine it with other things like telephone contact, informal meetings, social gatherings and a very driven approach to build and maintain relations in any way you can.

Get help influencing people
Once you have found out what you yourself can do to influence the people who have the key to accomodate your demands, then you can expand the field and look into whether additional individuals could also be of help. This is called influencing via a third party and it means, for example, that the stories other peope relate to your counterpart about you could be part of what will create the necessary concession. This is particularly interesting when we talk about negotiations for advancement, new assignments, more influence or status. Having investigated who your future negotiation counterparts will be, you may have found out that they are part of certain networks or informal groups where you

have no immediate access. The traditional conception that the most important deals are made 'behind closed doors' is perhaps not far off the mark. Even if you don't have access to these 'rooms' yourself, perhaps somebody else, who knows you as an ambitious and competent employee, does. They can pass on this perception of you in the fora where you are not invited. People in your network can also be called upon to assist you in influencing the right people in connection with a negotiation, where you need to be perceived as a valuable member of staff.

Mentor schemes can be a fantastic way to learn from more experienced professionals but also a chance to expand your network and get to know influential people well enough for them to be comfortable recommending you to others. Networks with female colleagues and connections have become very popular, and we often hear great examples of powerful women recommending and furthering other women's careers as well as sharing their particular knowledge and experience. One example of the importance of being part of this kind of network is related in former U.S. Secretary of State Madeleine Albright's autobiography *Madame Secretary*:

> Madeleine Albright talks about her time as an ambassador to the UN. She got together the few (only seven!) female UN-ambassadors in a network and they promised each other, that they would always answer the phone should one member of the group call another. A male ambassador from a larger EU country was rather provoked by the fact that the ambassadors from Liechtenstein or Barbados (both of them women) had this kind of direct access to the US ambassador. Madeleine Albright simply replied: "Well, you'll just have to choose a woman ambassador then!"

Apart from this type of network it pays off to seek out and include powerful men in the networks you build, because they will have access to different environments. It is apparently a fact that in order for a man to recommend a woman for a job, he needs to be 110% sure that she can make it. Convincing someone of this may take some time. Were he to recommend a man, he would be less worried as to whether the candidate lived up to his reputation, because a man would not be scrutinised as closely as a woman, especially when talking about a working environment where women are in the minority. Networking experts talk about how men tend to network with those in a higher position than themselves, whereas women get together with others at the same career level. In doing so, they don't use the advantages of networking to its full potential, especially when we're talking about advancing one's career. When we talk about possibilities for influencing decision-makers and people with power, then networks become important arenas where you can create important collaborations and alliances, plant some good ideas and signal what your particular interests and needs are. You will be able to start to shift the people you need to move towards you in a negotiation, and you will also build your reputation in general as someone to take notice of. All this means a lot once you start the actual negotiation.

Say what you want before the meeting
Your offers, objectives and demands must be communicated before the meeting in order to have time to influence your counterpart. As indicated by the framework shown earlier with the different suggested activities surrounding the actual meeting, I can strongly recommend that you say what you want before the meeting. "Help!", you may think "then they will have more time to find good reasons to say no to my demand!" Well, if they want to say no, they will also do so even if the first they hear of your demand is at the meeting, if not for any other reason than making sure that they don't promise you too much. In Appendix V you'll find an exercise that may help you preparing to make an ambitious first offer. You have to imagine the other person sitting at their work table preparing the negotiation. If there are no demands or offers from you in front of them but instead a couple of letters with demands from some of your colleagues, then it will be these demands that affect the counterpart and how they distribute what needs distributing. They may think: "I haven't heard from this person (you, that is) so she

is probably ok. Not so the others, so I probably won't be able to avoid giving them some kind of concessions." Basically this is all about how many different, small or large, measures will have a big effect and make your negotiations easier and less wrought with conflict. If you start early and make known well in advance of your meeting your demands and the (few, but good) arguments in support of your proposal as well as other helpful ideas, then your counterpart has a chance to be influenced by the things you have said and done in support of what you want. Then there won't be big surprises, raised eyebrows or shocked silences in the half hour you have scheduled for the meeting where an agreement needs to be made. The person you'll be negotiating with is probably doing the same thing to you, which might sound like this:

> You're having lunch with your boss the day before you have scheduled a meeting to agree on next year's budget for all departments. Your department's budget is in dire need of a substantial boost, and you are aiming to ask for a 20% increase. This is on your mind while your boss is talking more generally about how things are going. She then talks about the agreement she just made with one of your colleagues, who is head of another department, which happens to be a high profile part of the organisation. She mentions that unfortunately there was no extra funding for this department even though they have done an exeptionally good job over the last many months. The general economic situation is simply too critical. So, what will you ask for at your negotiation tomorrow?

It is almost impossible not to influence other people or be affected by them. By being aware of the possibilities inherent in this 'traffic' between human beings, then you can expand the arenas you negotiate in, both in time and space. It will enhance your chances to become very precise and strategic when you negotiate, and it will take the pressure off the meeting itself, which is the next thing we will work on.

✷ RECOMMENDED EXERCISES

Expand your possibilities for influencing your counterpart by making use of the time before and after the meeting itself. The movement towards agreement in negotiation happens when we as partakers of the process influence each other in order to reach a shared result.
Make a plan for what you will do, how and when.

Show your worth and your wishes on a regular basis: to those you'll be negotiating with and to the people they listen to. Let 'the story' of you and your results pave the way for a successfull negotiation.

Say what you want and be as clear as possible before the meeting itself, so the person who has the influence to grant your requests will have an opportunity to find ways of giving you what you want.

PHASE 3 – STRIKING THE DEAL

As if it wasn't enough to run around and prepare your negotiations, think about ambitious proposals, influencing relevant people and sowing seeds in all corners, the effort you must make to get a good deal is not quite over. At some point you usually sit down and strike the deal or make the agreement. This may happen on the telephone or over email, but we often choose the meeting as the forum in which to reach an agreement. Whoever facilitates a meeting has a lot of influence, and this is particularly true of negotiation meetings. By facilitating a meeting I mean designing and leading the meeting process, not simply managing the list of speakers or taking minutes. When taking on the task of planning this meeting and how it is held you can work specifically to change many of the less favourable conditions that might apply in certain working environments. If one of these terms are, that women often hold back their demands or make too modest demands, then one way of structuring for instance a meeting where funds are allocated could be to make sure that everybody gets an equal opportunity to speak at the meeting and state their demands. Perhaps you as facilitator has made it a structured part of the preparation for all the participants at the meeting to hand in requests well in advance, to prevent invisible power structures from determining who gets something and who doesn't. An example of how effective it can be to decide to facilitate or lead the negotiation meeting in a focused and constructive way is this story I heard from a course participant:

> This woman was going to negotiate with a counterpart she knew from previous occasions. Those earlier meetings had almost always ended in a dead-lock and became marathons of arguments and heavy discussions which didn't get them anywhere. As part of our negotiation course she had been asked to try the very central technique of asking good questions as opposed to listing endless arguments in support of *her* view. She decided to test this at these difficult negotiation meetings, and she stuck to her plan and steered clear of the usual dead-lock by always reverting to 'interview-mode' whenever they encountered obstacles. The meeting was a huge success and contrary to expectations they managed to reach an agreement without any bruises or black eyes. Her counterpart then asked her: "What happened here?" and looked quizzically at our negotiator. She chose to tell her what she had done, which the other party found very thought provoking and a valuable lesson.

Starting the meeting

Most people are used to and quite comfortable starting a meeting with some initial small talk. You talk about how things are going, what the weather has been like or current affairs in business or politics. Because negotiation for most people are associated with something they find difficult and which can make them nervous, it is of the utmost importance for the further process to get off to a good start. To build a relation with mutual trust is quite central to most negotiations, especially when talking about parties that meet continually. Trust comes from showing mutual respect, recognising each other's point of view as legitimate and avoiding personal attacks. A picture of how you can work purposefully on strengthening your relationship with the person you negotiate with is the image of someone scouring the ground with a metal detector looking for gold, that is; looking for something you like about the other person or find interesting. You let the detector sweep across the ground, and when it beeps, you start digging! If you specifically and consistently look for what you actually like or approve of, even agree with in the counterpart's personality, viewpoints or suggestions and ideas and then zoom in on this, then you create very favourable conditions for strengthening a positive relation. If you start out aiming to build trust and create as positive conditions as possible for reaching an agreement, then it also becomes clearer what you need to do in order to support this. In a meeting framework this is all about planning and facilitating a process that supports the wish to reach an agreement that is as advantageous as possible for both parties.

In a negotiation it is therefore even more important to think about the order of which you do things, so you won't encounter unnecessary resistance simply because you might not have the patience to smalltalk with your counterpart or have forgotten to provide coffee and croissants for an early meeting, things which in themselves are strong signals of how important you find this meeting, and how prepared you are to accomodate somebody.

> A seasoned negotiator told me once about some very complex, difficult and drawn-out negotiations for large contracts on industrial hardware he conducted in several Baltic countries. There was never anything to eat or drink at the long and arduous meetings; no coffee or tea, nothing to eat, not even a glass of water. As the meetings often went on for hours, he decided in the end to bring along a picnic basket full of food and drink, thereby making sure that they had an occasional break and that all participants got the necessary energy to finish the work.

So forget all about the old 'tricks' that people like to suggest, partly joking, where you leave your counterpart with the light in their eyes, in a lower chair than yourself or with the heating turned up too high, hungry or thirsty. If your purpose is to encourage people to make a good and lasting agreement with you, if this is what you hope to achieve, then you must make sure that they have the optimal conditions for doing so.

> **Consider** if you can take on the role of host. Make sure the meeting takes place in a comfortable environment and provide some refreshments.
>
> **Have the patience** to do some smalltalking and use this opportunity to get to know each other (even) better and to build trust by taking an interest in your counterpart's world thus appreciating who they are and strengthening their legitimacy.
>
> **Agree** on the framework for the negotiation: How much time do you have, what are you aiming to get through today, in what sequence or order will you work through it, what information and material is available, where can you go for time-outs etc. etc.

Wishes and demands first
When the coffee cups are empty and the anecdotes from a recent holiday have been told, then there is no getting around what most people find the hardest part of the negotiation: To say what it is you want. You *know* that the other person doesn't want the same as you, but say it you must, in order for you to be able to start working on finding a solution. Here I would like to repeat the advice on exchanging demands *before* the meeting, so both parties have had time to think about where to give concessions and which parts are too important to let go. A young manager in a big company gave her own good advice on how to prepare yourself for presenting your demand without blinking:

> "When I prepare myself for a negotiation and think about what I want and what my demand will be, then I always decide that *I won't blush until I'm back outside the door*! To allow myself to be ambitious but at the same time recognise, in advance, that this can be very difficult and almost embarrassing helps me when I sit facing the people I negotiate with."

To present your wishes and proposals demands a certain control of the process and the way in which you communicate. When you hear what the other person says and realise that their demand is different from yours – it is good to remember that we as human beings have a tendency to focus on what we *disagree* with in what the other person says and the risks this involves.

> What is being said:
> "We can't give you the increase in budget for your project that you asked for, because for now we have chosen to prioritise projects with a more visible output. The other thing you mentioned about a possible future reorganisation of assignments in order to lighten the load on your staff we can probably do, but you will not get extra funding for more staff."

> What you hear:
> "No money for my important project – they don't appreciate the work we do! No help to deal with the extra workload – they don't care that we're all stressed out! It's simply just not fair"

Our ears are tuned into hearing all the 'nos' we expect to find because this is a negotiation, and we know that there will be resistance. The disadvantage of being disposed to hear all the rejections in the answer is that the 'yes'es' hidden in the reply are neither heard nor recognised or acted upon. In the above example one could also choose to focus on and ask about the following:

What you could say:
"You're saying 'for now', what does that mean? How and when do you decide on the distribution of funds for projects? You mention the need for visible outputs, what does this entail? What will it take for my project to enter into this category? The reorganisation and redistribution of assignments with a view to lightening the load for the staff is important, so how do we proceed from here? What are your thoughts on this? What will it take for you to be able to consider giving me extra funding for additional staff?"

Instead of clamping down on all the no's you hear, you can also choose to look for and closely examine the hints of a yes or the signs of an opening from the others. It will be two very different conversations depending on whether you start off by discussing all your points of disagreements, or if you choose to make a note of all the points of agreement you can possibly find. You can almost sense how the atmosphere, and not least the optimism about reaching an agreement, is enhanced by starting off by talking about all the things you already agree on or where you are close to finding a solution. The trick is to be prepared for the no, to expect it. If you simply got a yes, this might also be perceived negatively ("This was too easy, I should have asked for more"). The interesting challenge you are faced with is to find ways to transform this 'no' to a 'yes' or a 'maybe' or even a 'not now but perhaps later'.

Examining the disagreements

Most of us do not like to disagree with others and we are easily affected emotionally by a no. It is important to examine and do some sorting of the no's in order to achieve two things. Firstly, to discover all the actual and potential yes'es that are hiding behind and in-between the no's (a no to a payrise may hide a yes to a paid training course). Secondly, to realise that in some aspects the parties simply perceive the world in different ways and that this is okay (agreeing on how to lead an organisation might not be necessary in order to agree in a negotiation about wages and working conditions). If you are able to put the views and attitudes you don't agree with on hold and focus instead on the hidden yes'es, then you may be able to reach agreement. Being angry or upset that the person sitting across from you do not understand that you are right, could tempt you to start hauling out all the arguments that support your view and start bombarding the other person with these, hoping to change the way they see the world. But as I have mentioned earlier, arguments rarely produce agreements if they stand alone. They have to be tested for efficiency; do they actually work? This you do by asking questions:

> "We have to solve the problem of a too heavy workload for the staff, as we otherwise risk people becoming ill with stress. What are your thoughts on this? Do you have any suggestions as to how we proceed from here? What has worked in other departments? What can we do ourselves within the department to help you find the extra funding needed to hire more staff?"

The trick is to hold back your irritation and start working as an investigative journalist would. What you are looking for is a path that leads to what you want, meaning that you will be working with the person you negotiate with to try and change the no to a yes. You will be looking for the interests behind the demands made by the negotiators in order to start getting ideas and finding ways to reach a solution that will satisfy both parties' needs. To ask your counterpart questions, even though this person's views differ from yours, will also have a highly positive and relationship-building effect, because they will feel listened to and acknowledged. This is a very basic need in most of us, and research have shown that this aspect is particularly important when deciding *if* we want to negotiate at all, and *how* we interpret the results. To listen to what your counterpart has to say is not the same as agreeing. But it will open up for mutual interest and respect, and the answers you get can enhance your understanding of the other party and indicate possible ways to move forwards. A communications adviser (and former journalist) puts it like this:

"A lot of people think that as long as my arguments are good enough, then that's all I need. You spend all your time and energy preparing and refining them, and then just assuming that the other person understands that you are right. Instead you could say: I sense that you don't quite agree? Why is that? I'm a journalist, so to be curious about other people, their thoughts, actions and choices is incredibly important – and it works!"

On some occasions you may encounter more resistance to yourself and your demands than at other times. This can be both a surprise and put you off, so here are some suggestions as to what you can do if the person you negotiate with hits below the belt or attacks you right out. These concrete tools are inspired by Deborah Kolb's thoughts on 'Strategic Moves and Turns' from her book *The Shadow Negotiation*:

To ask about what you hear; examine what the other person means, make sure you understand it the way it is intended – this can make the unreasonable part of their behaviour quite obvious. Be careful to avoid hypothetical questions like: "So, what you're really saying is that I'm not good enough?" – which is more an accusation than a question, and it can spark off a fruitless discussion. Ask instead: "What competencies and qualifications do you find relevant here?"

Reformulation: Get the process back on track by reformulating what was said in more neutral terms and with a focus on the content. "You obviously don't know what you're talking about" becomes: "I suggest we examine the facts in more detail?"

Make space: If a counterpart is angry or emotional, then let this person finish talking, listen and recognise that this is important for them. Be attentive, but stop them if the tone or language becomes offensive

Put the process on hold: If the tone of voice is unpleasant or not constructive, then ask for a break encouraging all participants to continue thinking about how to proceed, and then continue the process later and in a different tone.

Build up your mandate: Demonstrate that you have influence and mandate as a negotiator, if your counterpart don't see you as such and this creates an imbalance. Make it clear that you are dependent on each other for making an agreement

Ideas create possibilities for making deals

As part of interviewing your counterpart you can make a conscious effort to get new ideas, that will satisfy the interests you hear the other person has. We have already talked about how it makes sense to 'expand the pie' before you start sharing it. In this way you have a bigger chance of everybody getting a sizeable share, but this expansion will only happen if you choose to spend some time finding the extra things that will enable you to increase the volume of the deal. It is often hard to get to this point, if your time together is spent presenting arguments and counterarguments to each other. When you talk to competent, professional business negotiators, who deal with complex agreements like contracts in big mergers between companies, then you quickly notice that what they spend most of their time doing, is finding alternative solutions to the problems they encounter. As soon as they encounter an obstacle they start thinking about and working to find new ways to ensure that all parties are as happy as possible. In mergers of all types, being able to work together after the negotiation is extremely important, and professional negotiators know, that pressuring or forcing the parties to agree might jeopardise the agreements in the end.

The agreement – to strike a deal

Now we have reached the phase where images of used-cars salesmen or horsetraders in a marketplace emerge in our minds. And this is not all wrong, because once you have investigated and discovered the parties' demands and the interests behind, you will have some good ideas as to how to expand the field, include more aspects in your agreement and only then is it time to strike a deal. Now comes the time where it is of utmost importance that the negotiators both are willing to move. This is when you have to be able to give concessions where it matters the least in exchange for something of value to you. To strike a deal might sound like this:

> "I understand that you need to reduce pressure on your staff. So *if* you agree to *share* a person with two other departments instead of hiring someone fulltime for your department only, *then* we will look into the possibilities of relieving your department of some of the tasks you have now. We can't increase your budget, at least not at the moment."

> "This sounds good, but *if* I'm to accept sharing a co-worker with other departments, *then* this person must be placed physically in our department, and we need to get the lion's share of the available time; 25 hours. Being relieved of some of our tasks will need to be agreed upon within the month, and then I'd like to have a provisional agreement that funds will be found for the project within the next three months. *If* all this is in place, *then* we have a deal."

> "Okay, *if* we agree to your demands regarding the extra member of staff, *then* redistributing some of your tasks can't be that urgent. We will look into this within three months, and we can agree provisionally to inviting you to negotiate for a part of the extra funding as soon as this money may be found."

> "It's a deal!"

Two little words are important here, because they ensure that you get something in return for what you give. This is a trade, not a sell-out. When you use the words 'if' and 'then', you make sure that the concession you have in mind will be compensated for with something from the other side of the table. You constantly give a little but with a keen view to getting something in return. This is a way to secure a balaced deal and that both parties feel they get 'something'.

Time-outs create movement

Within the framework of the defining meeting where the deal is struck, it is strongly recommended to arrange for time-outs or breaks. As a negotiator it is your responsibility to make sure that the agreement you reach is as good as possible. There are many things you can use a time-out for:

> **If you have become angry**, surprised or in some other way distracted, then you can regain your balance by getting out of the room, get some air, talk to the people you may be negotiating in a team with, call someone for advice and support etc.

> **You can spend the break getting ideas** for how to proceed, thinking of more questions you need to ask in order to discover the 'gold' that will enable you to proceed, or you can do the maths and make sure you know the economic consequences of deals you may be about to strike. You can recap and do a status of how things are going, both content- and process-wise.

> **During the time-out** it will probably be possible for you to talk to your counterpart in a less formal manner. This phenomenon has been made into a ritual in certain areas (union-management negotiations, political negotiations). Perhaps it is easier for your counterpart to give you concessions outside the formal meeting environment?

> **Fresh air, something to eat, an actual break** from it all can give you the necessary energy and courage to proceed. To hope that by exhausting the other person and making tiredness and hunger push them to sign may result in them regretting the deal

they made, once they have regained their strength. This will make them less willing to stick to the agreement, and it will certainly make them prepare for the worst before they meet you again.

It is a paradox, that the greatest movement towards an agreement often happens when the parties are on a time-out or a break. When you leave the meeting room and each other, knowing that you need to make a deal at some point, then the parties will spend the time thinking about how to get the process going again, where to give concessions and where to stay firm etc. So don't be nervous about taking a time-out in a negotiation, but explain why you need it: " I would really like to make a deal with you, but your bid is too low. So I need some time to think about this and consider how we can proceed from here." The other person is left with the message that there is hope of a deal, but that it will take a little more to reach it, and that both parties will need to find something. This will make the negotiators go back to work on the deal and, when you meet the next time, something has almost always changed, a movement has occurred. When you negotiate there may be many things on the agenda, and it can be difficult to keep a clear picture of what is going on, especially if you do as recommended and 'expand the pie' with many new ideas and suggestions. Taking notes and writing things down throughout the negotiation is strongly advised, even if the other person has the 'official' responsibility for taking down the minutes of the meeting. It is a way of managing the speed of the process. You may ask questions such as: "Do I understand correctly that your major obstacle is finding sufficient funding? And that for this reason you would rather contribute with manpower to this project?" If you make notes along the way, then you will pause more often and check your understanding. This is both a message to your counterpart that you are listening, and it will reduce the risk of misunderstandings, that might complicate things later.

The final agreement
At last you place the final full stop on the deal. This is when it needs to be written down, confirmed and cheering is in order. When you have

come this far, perhaps through a tough and turbulent process, then most people are keen to finish. It may be a great temptation to speed things up when the finishing line is in sight. Sometimes you sense, that the deal may be a little bit wobbly, and this may make you want to hurry on out of the room saying: "Well that's agreed, then, right? I'm off, take care" choosing to let sleeping dogs lie and without having had time to make sure, that the deal is actually made, that is; the deal that you hope to have made. In negotiations, as in many other situations, people hear mostly what they would *like* to hear. This is not from ill will, but it means that it is a very good idea to have patience and a steady hand, when you reach the end of the negotiation process.

Make time to go over what you have agreed upon, item by item. If you find that you disagree on what you agreed on ("Oh no no, this is not at all what we agreed on!"), then stop and see, if you can make a quick adjustment and agree, or if you need to put this point on hold, in order to go through the rest of the agreement. As with the start of the negotiation, where the sensible thing to do is to focus on where you already agree, I clearly recommend that you don't allow yourself to be unnecessarily provoked if the other party has a different view of the deal you just made. It is tempting to think: "That's typical, they always cheat, and I bet they didn't think I would notice." Perhaps the misunderstanding was on purpose, perhaps not. But it will not benefit the negotiation to flare up and accuse your counterpart of cheating. Give them the benefit of the doubt and return to the points in the agreement you still need to settle, and use the same procedure as before: What is it we both want here? More ideas to help us move forward? What can I bargain with here?

★ RECOMMENDED EXERCISES

Make sure the meeting starts well, make room for small-talk and agree on the framework for the negotiation.

Start by hearing demands and proposals from both parties. Interview each other in order to investigate viewpoints and interests, and don't get angry if you don't immediately agree. If you did agree, you wouldn't be negotiating.

Keep a keen look out for possible agreements, small or large. Investigate these and make sure to 'harvest' them before you start working on the more difficult issues.

Create more ideas, on your own or with your counterpart as to how you can proceed. Get help from others on how to 'expand the pie' before you divide it. The more substance you negotiate about, the easier it will be to meet everybody's interests and needs.

Strike some deals that ensure a fair share for all parties involved. Use the words 'if' and 'then' to make sure, that the deal is balanced ("If I'm to give you this, then you must give me that"). Write down all the points you agree on along the way.

PHASE 4 – AFTER THE MEETING

As I have mentioned before, most negotiators are relieved and happy once they have reached a good agreement. You may be exhausted and just needing to get on with your life, so once you have signed the papers and finished your coffee, it's out of sight and out of mind. When negotiators leave each other, they also start the process of interpreting the deal they have just made.

// RESEARCH ON... TO REACH A GREAT RESULT

When is a result great? Or simply good enough? Recently social psychologists have tried to develop a method to measure the subjective value of a negotiation result in order to get a more detailed picture of the mere objective content. It is in fact very central to a satisfactory negotiation, that you have a good feeling about your own participation in the process and about the content of the agreement. As we can never quite know what an objectively great result is (your counterpart hopefully won't tell you that "you could have gotten much more out of me!") then hearing what the individual negotiator's intuitive and subjective rating is, is the best we can do. A subjective evaluation of results includes looking at how good the actual content is and, in addition, looking at how you perceive yourself as part of the negotiation, the process itself and your relations to your counterpart. The interesting thing is that the questions you ask yourself in order to evaluate a result will, for example, relate to what degree you have been able to act according to your personal values (have you had the chance to convey the essence of you without having been forced into a defensive position or having lost face?); if you have been listened to and appreciated, and how much you trust your counterpart and consequently feel like meeting again and negotiating. These are all aspects of the negotiation, which will be affected by the way you behave, the way you communicate and respect each other as negotiating partners. These aspects will influence the perception you have of the actual content of the agreement, so there are extremely good reasons to work on making the negotiation process as constructive as possible instead of focusing exclusively on content. You can test how happy you are with a negotiation result on :www.subjectivevalue.com

(Source: Daniel T. Gilbert, et al., The Wisdom in Feeling: Psychological Processes in Emotional Intelligence)

Appreciate the agreement

Understandably most people need a break after closing a deal, but now is the time for the agreement to try its wings in the real world, and this is why it is important to follow up on what you have agreed on. Both parties have given concessions throughout the negotiation, which makes it vital to make sure that the agreement is honoured even if your counterpart may meet resistance and criticism when they are back in their own environment talking to 'their' people, who might also be affected by the deal.

If someone has given you something, it is always a good idea to say 'Thank you'. It is also a good idea to show that the decision they have made to give you something was the right one to make. This is why you need to be in close contact with your negotiation counterpart in the time following the signing of the agreement. It might look like this:

> You meet your boss, who has given you a substantial payrise and a bonus after long and tough negotiations. She looks a bit preoccupied, but you get a chance to chat with her and you tell her how happy you are with the negotiation the two of you had. You stress how much better it feels to have been lifted to the same level as the other experts in the organisation, and the improvement in your finances has made things easier at home to everyone's relief.

If someone is to give concessions in a negotiation, they need to know that it matters. If there is no feedback after the meeting - everything continues as normal and your boss remains unaware of what she gave you has meant to you – well, then she might not see the point of giving you anything next time around. In talking about your recent negotiation you are sowing the seeds for the next one, which means that – in effect – as a negotiator, you never have time off, the process goes on interminably.

★ RECOMMENDED EXERCISES

Say thank you when your counterpart gives you something. Evaluate the process, so you both make sure to keep working in ways that are conducive to the negotiation (a clear framework for the process, enough time, being attentive and showing respect, producing good ideas and suggestions etc.)

Agree with your counterpart how the deal will live on; who says what to whom, how do you make sure the deal holds etc.

Keep in touch in the time following the negotiation and confirm with your counterpart, that what she gave you has had the promised effect. Look ahead to future negotiations with optimism and continue the effective, day-to-day work of influencing each other.

THE PARALLEL NEGOTIATION

If we wish to change the conditions we negotiate under, there are a number of areas to start working on. One of these is the parallel negotiation, where we signal to the surroundings how we see ourselves and how we would like to be perceived by others. In this negotiation you can work on improving your impact and mandate, on influencing and facilitating the process steering it in a positive direction, and you can work on strengthening the collaboration with the people you surround yourself with (who will also be, at some stage or other, the persons you negotiate with!). The following exchange I found in the novel by Stieg Larsson *The Girl Who Kicked the Hornet's Nest* (original version) where the protagonist, an investigative journalist Michael Blomkvist, has arrived at a meeting with the head of Constitutional Protection, a department of the Swedish police. Apart from the head of the department and Michael Blomkvist two male and one female police, Monica Figuerola, are present. Michael Blomkvist is talking to the head, Torsten Edklinth (excerpt from the original version, my translation):

> "Where do we start?" Michael asked.
> "How would you like to start with some coffee…Monica?"
> "Yes please!" Monica Figuerola said.
> Michael noticed that the head of Constitutional Protection hesitated for a moment, before he got up to get the thermos with coffee and brought it to the meetingroom table, where cups were

already in place. Torsten Edklinth had probably meant for Monica Figuerola to serve the coffee. Michael also noted, that Edklinth smiled to himself, which Michael took as a good sign.
(Stieg Larsson, *Luftslottet som sprängdes*)

In a very elegant manner Monica Figuerola returns to sender an obviously discriminating remark, causing him to become aware of his unfortunate behaviour. Nothing is said, but in the parallel negotiation of her status and power Monica Figuerola has demonstrated both selfconfidence and that she expects to be treated fairly. She signals very clearly how she would like to be perceived, and it is exactly these small, but very central and symbolic acts, that have a great impact in the parallel negotiation.

The parallel negotiation takes place every time we meet another person and it very much influences the actual negotiations we will have with others – but it is often unspoken or even unconscious, which is what makes it parallel. Nevertheless it is extremely important because it will play a part in either making the negotiation process go smoothly or perhaps get derailed. It is impossible to know exactly what upsets others or what they find positive. This is why the best you can really do is trying to be the person you would most want to be; that is to find out what signals you would like to send out, how you would like others to percieve you? It is important to be comfortable with who you are, so you can relax and focus on what you are in the process of doing – that is, working towards an agreement.

How to dress and body language

There is no doubt that our physical appearance and the clothes we wear will form part of the impression others get of us. Women tend to have a wider palette to work with, especially when we talk about relations at work where in most places there are various, generally accepted ways to dress. This can be an advantage, but it also means that women are noticed more, which lends extra meaning into the way we dress. In negotiation one would think that everything is determined by cold facts, and that the content of an agreement can be measured and weighed in a neutral manner. But mutual trust and sympathy, a good atmosphere and respectful behaviour as well as our personal appearance and tone of voice are all things that affect both the process and the result. This is why the way we dress is also a part of the equation. If you are comfortable using yourself and your body as a means to influence someone, there is nothing wrong with that. But it is a very 'loaded' tool to use, and one you can never be sure of the effect of, so it must be used after careful consideration. Flirting and behaving in a provocative way can become an Achilles Heel if you, as part of your negotiation, also wish to build up respect around the professional you, to get the reputation of being a serious negotiator and hope to minimize the filter created through gender. What 'provocative' means here I think most people have a sense of themselves, and choosing this kind of behaviour will no doubt affect both your body language and the way you communicate. As the gender researcher Karen Sjørup pointed to in the chapter on gender, you might end up needing to do some 'repair-work', if focus has been on, for example, your physical appearance and even flirting, which makes me think that using this is all about dosage. It is there, we can't eliminate the physical impressions from the negotiations (unless we use other media, of course) but being aware of the effect our body language and dress might have on others will give us the possibility to adjust this effect when negotiating with a counterpart. You may signal a great many things with your body language. In negotiation the recommendation is to create an atmosphere of mutual respect and trust. But, as significant, it is important to create an atmosphere where the parties feel they have a mandate and that there is weight behind their wishes and demands. This is shown by the way you enter a room, how you sit either relaxed and comfortably in your chair or straightbacked and tightly against the edge of the table. You need to find ways of signalling the kind of influence and impact you would like to have.

> **How do you enter a room?** Do you skulk along the walls, or do you meet your counterpart face on and shake their hands? Smile? Stop and chat?

Do you have eye contact with everyone at the table? Are you sitting comfortably, ready to work?

What do you do during a break? Clear the room and get some fresh coffee? Open the windows and making a quick call to check everything's ok at home? Or do you look up your counterpart and continue the negotiation in the hallway?

Communication

The way we speak, our voices and the things we say will affect the parallel negotiation. Do you speak too fast or even too much? Or slowly, concisely and in brief statements?

A male journalist/editor admitted, hard pressed, at a public meeting about the media's limited use of women experts, that one of the reasons journalists will more often contact a male expert on a particular topic is that they are better at delivering short, precise statements. They are very to-the-point and are not afraid to put an edge on what they say, even though it may provoke some people. Not so the women experts, the editor said. In his experience, women would use many more words and longer sentences in trying to modify, justify and make relevant their viewpoints – which makes it all too long and imprecise.

It's a worrying story but also quite enlightening, because what kind of a signal are we sending as women experts if we need so many words and so much 'wrapping' when we make statements in the media? Short precise statements signal assuredness, that you know what you are talking about and that you are quite firm in your viewpoint. The problem about being very short and concise and thereby seemingly selfassured as a woman could be the filter you are perceived through, where there are hidden and probably unconscious prejudices about how women ought not to be too self-assured and therefore can be judged more harshly than their male colleagues. I think there is a reason why we as women sometimes tend to 'cushion' what we say with explanations and reservations. You sense that by being too selfassured and straightforward in your statements, you might provoke someone when laying out the text for them. It can sound very harsh if a woman gets up and says: "This is how it is, so there is nothing to discuss." Instead you might end up saying: "I'm pretty sure that this is how things are, even though you could perhaps argue the opposite. So, if it were up to me, I still think this is the direction we should take, but then again, we can always ask the others, or what do you think?" Longwinded and insecure, indeed, so the middle road could be the following sentence, which is meant to signal both knowledge and selfassuredness, but without being too confrontational or too vague: "My experience tells me, that this is how it is. What else do you need to know in order to trust me on this?" A rule of thumb is: Be clear about what you think, but follow up with a question that will invite the other to come your way, because we are still talking about negotiation here, albeit a parallel and perhaps unspoken one, and the way we communicate is a mirror of how we see ourselves. We can (and should) use the way we communicate to signal both robustness and flexibility: I'm confident about my own experience and knowledge, but I'm also interested to know how you think. So, keep a close eye on the signals that lie in different ways of communicating:

> **Do you wrap up your statements too much?** A long prologue and many arguments or explanations or perhaps even modifications?
>
> **Do you devalue or modify the impact of what you say** with words like: 'A little bit, perhaps, by any chance, if that's ok' etc.?
>
> **How do you best and most distinctively signal your power** and professionalism with your language? Try out different versions of a statement on a friend, and find the version you like best. Find out *why* it works.

When I interviewed the head of a section of the Danish Security and Intelligence Service, I found a very good example of what it means to be able to express yourself clearly and concisely. During a number of years this head of section had had some media training, which has made her able to express herself in short, precise sentences and still get her message through:

> "I know that I only have 30 seconds, so I think things through in advance: "What is my key message? And how do I make clear enough so even my grandmother would be able to understand it?"

This particular woman often has to communicate and explain very complex issues in a very short time and to a very broad audience. This doesn't mean that she has simplified her message to the extent that she talks down to the viewers, but rather that she uses statements and short sentences that you can hear she has thought through. Apart from being a very competent communicator, she also generally spends a lot of time asking questions and finding out how others view a particular problem. By doing both, she manages to demonstrate great competence and knowledge in her field, which positions her in the parallel negotiation as a person with both power and mandate. Her inquisitiveness invites others to take part in the conversation and take the edge of whatever hidden prejudice about competent and clear-spoken women the listener might have.

An awful lot of the communication at work takes place in meetings, formal as well as informal ones. Many meetings are quite unstructured and shamble along haphazardly and people tend to describe this as 'talking things through' or 'discussing something'. When there is no one leading the meeting process and there is no one who structures who speaks when and in what framework, then it will often be the ones who talk the most, the loudest and for the longest time, that will influence the subject matter. Research shows that men talk more than women, both at work and at home. This doesn't mean that they are cleverer or more important, but in the parallel negotiation about power and position it does mean something if you participate actively and get your word in. One way of making sure that the word is shared more fairly is to take responsibility for facilitating, or leading the meeting process, for example, by saying: "How about I facilitate this meeting, so we get to hear everyone's wishes and wants? And that we then spend some time looking into what motivates people's demands, so we all know where we're coming from?" Again focus is on the process, and by taking on the design and leadership of a meeting process you can ensure that it will be a constructive one. In this way you get access to using the negotiation 'phases' we have talked about if the meeting has the objective of ending up with some kind of agreement or concensus. To be the facilitator should not be misused to give yourself the floor for most of the time, but neither does it mean that you should simply 'manage' the word and take minutes. It means guiding the participants through a constructive process you know works. At the same time, this will underpin your authority, make you very visible and give you a chance to manifest your mandate in the parallel negotiation.

★ RECOMMENDED EXERCISES

Consider how you would like to be perceived at work; as a colleague, employee, boss, collaborator, negotiator. What do you do in the parallel negotiation to support this image? Is there something you wold like to do more? Or less?

Body language, communcation and the way you dress all influence the parallel negotiation. The more relaxed and satisfied you are with your 'performance', the more free you will be to navigate and position yourself and manifesting your mandate and power. Get feedback from people you trust, and ask to know what works best.

Look at the way you participate in meetings and whether this behaviour gives you respect and influence. Take the initiative to lead, to facilitate the meetings, so you and the other participants experience a good and constructive process. To be a facilitator can give you the arena in which to demonstrate your power and position.

CHAPTER 5

NEGOTIATIONS AT HOME

NEGOTIATIONS AT HOME

Some time ago I read an article about a woman, who had taken early retirement as a result of a stress induced illness. Her description of the time leading up to her final break-down contained a story about how she was utterly overcome with the job of looking after her home. She realised this on one particular day, when she opened the door to her childrens' room and simply made a note of the fact that there were so many things, clothes and just general clutter, that they would not be able to make their way to their beds. "Well, then they will just have to make themselves a path through the mess", she thought and closed the door. This example was meant to illustrate the powerlessness and sheer exhaustion the woman felt, but what seemed striking to me was: At what point in time did it become this woman's sole responsibility that the house was clean, and the result of it not being so a factor in her succumbing to stress? What happened at the negotiation (with her partner and children) where she was landed with the full package of looking after the house?

There are differences in both *what* we negotiate and *how* we negotiate things at work and at home. There is also a difference in whether we even notice that we negotiate, and how we relate to the idea of negotiation when working and in our private lives. Many people think of negotiation as something rather formal and perhaps even ritual (wage negotiations, commercial deals etc.) and this makes the word somehow unsuitable for use in the private sphere. To use the word 'negotiation' might indicate that now we become two formal opponents, and that the good and close personal relationship takes second place. A woman told me, that her partner had asked her quite earnestly not to constantly say:"Can we negotiate this?" or "I think we should negotiate this". It seemed wrong to him to use this word as they were partners and in their own home. The woman told me, with a wry smile, that she had agreed to this request from her partner. However, she continued to negotiate – that is, to find acceptable solutions for both parties when things didn't just solve themselves. The example shows that it is less important what we call it, but a really good idea that we do it. That is, use negotiation as a tool to reach agreements not just at work but also at home, where there is often even more at stake. The stressed out woman from the article could perhaps have benefited from discovering that there were plenty of things to negotiate, and to make sure that agreements about who does what at home would include people other than just herself.

Project manager at home
In the January 2007 issue of The Economic Journal, researcher Hélène Couprie shares some results of studies she made about division of labour in couples, drawing on data from the British Household Panel Survey. Interestingly, single women in Britain spend 10 hours on average on housework whereas single men only spend 7 hours. However, when men and women get together and live as a couple, men's share of housework drops to 5 hours per week and that of women increases to 15 hours on average. She calls this 'a specialisation of labour' and explores the link between inequality in the private and public sphere. This 'specialisation' in housework may explain why women accumulate fewer skills in the labour market and why they may choose to lower their hours in the workplace, thus fuelling the wage gap. Fewer hours of work might also work negatively the other way around, as differences in working hours and thereby income is a major factor, when it comes to deciding who does what at home.

A Danish expert on labour relations, Agi Csonka, talks about some of the results of a study she made in 2004 about the balance between work life/private life and stress among Danish couples, and her conclusion is that:

> "It is often the women who have the responsibility for cooking, picking up the children etc. The men might help, but the women have the main responsibility and this is a stress factor. [...] It is also characteristic, that it often will be the women who adjust

their working life accordingly with the result, that they more often than men experience an imbalance in their working life. This leads to an increase in stress levels."

She also talks about how important it is to look at who is 'in charge' at home – that is: who is the project manager? Who is responsible for organising the family's social events? Scheduling the available hours to meet everyone's wishes and demands? And could this role be shared differently? Her point is that not only do women take on more of the actual household work, women also feel *responsible*, which only adds to the pressure of this role.

There are many nuances and different ways of looking at the division of labour at home, but numerous studies show a clear tendency that there is an imbalance in the distribution of housework, which also directly impacts worklife and career. So, if this applies to you, looking at how to get this back on track is perhaps a good place to start. As an important part of this work it is also necessary to look at the advantages connected to being the family project manager. What does it mean for you, that this responsibility also gives a certain control? How to tap into the very useful competence that most family project managers have; a great overview of things and the ability to make things happen, in this most vital jobs of all: to right the imbalance at home? Appendix VI contains a simple exercise with a focus on how your balance between work, household duties, leisure activities and time for yourself is distributed.

PHASE I: WHAT DO YOU WANT?

We have gone back to square one and will begin with the most important negotiation of all: the one you have with yourself about what you want to achieve. As in the workplace negotiations, this is all about thinking things through and becoming aware of the following:

How do you spend your time at home?
What do you do?
What jobs do you do, and how long do they take you?
What do you think about these jobs – do you enjoy doing them?
What are your feelings about having to do them? Does it seem fair?
How is the balance between duties and fun?
How would you like it to be?
Is the responsibility for, and the housework itself, fairly and equally shared?

Get an overview

It is important to get an overview of how things actually are before you can start changing things, and also to look at why you might have ended up in an imbalanced situation. When talking about the distribution of housework it is easy to fall into an almost habitual complaint that "It's always me who has to do everything! I'm fed up that you don't carry your share of the load" etc. But when you look closely at how this situation came to be, perhaps you may find that some of the responsibility lies with yourself. As the woman in the article about stress, you do have a choice when you distribute the workload at home. You can clench your jaw and get on with it. Slam the door to the dishwasher and develop a continuous monologue about how unfair things are in the vain hope that, whoever this speech is directed at, hears it. Just as we in the workplace would like to be noticed and appreciated, rewarded and praised for the work we do, you also want credit for the things you do at home. But you need to *ask for* what you want also in this case. It won't help to place the full responsibility for an imbalance in the sharing of housework on the one that does the least. The partners who are freewheeling or only consider themselves obliged to 'help' only do this because they have been given the possibility to do so.

It can be difficult sorting through the things with which you fill your life because this sorting involves a lot of feelings. But, as in all negotiation, getting an overview of the facts is a great starting point for change.

Spend some time becoming clear about what you spend your days doing, and find out if you think the balance is right. If not, then perhaps this is a good time to negotiate a new division of labour with the people with whom you share your life; partners, children, family and friends. A relatively simple way of getting this overview is drawing 'The well' – a drawing that uses the image of a well as a symbol of how you feel at a given time. There is a certain level of water in the well, and this indicates how much energy and happiness you feel at this point in time. A high water level indicates a surplus of energy and that you fill your life with things and people that make you happy. A low level is an image of feeling drained and tired and with very little energy and joy. You start by trying to feel what level the water in your well is at right now, and make that line on your drawing of the well. Stop and think for a moment about the level in the well: Is this really how things are? And are you happy with this? The next step is to think about and investigate what makes you happy? What gives you energy and strength? What makes sense in your world and is of great value to you? Write this list of things on one side of the well, indicating that it is from this you can fill your well. On the other side of the well, you describe what drains the well: What taps your energy and makes you stressed? What feels heavy to do and like a burden? In this way you will make a list of things, that you might want to minimize in order to prevent all the good energy and happiness from constantly disappearing from your well. A 'well' might look like this:

Hanging out with the family
Reading a good book
Running with my friend

Energy
Contentment
Joy

Too many meetings with clients
Duty dinners with other couples
Gardening

This exercise was used on a leadershiptraining course I taught with Michael Day, CEO of Historic Royal Palaces in the UK. He made the participants think about this as a vital part of finding out what would make them even better leaders and more balanced people, and it always turned out to be a very intense and revealing process. To look at your life from a distance and think about the things that give you energy and what drains you could be the first step towards making the decision to negotiate your way to more of the good stuff and less of the bad.

What can you negotiate?

When we look at our personal lives the most obvious negotiation is the one about how to share the most ordinary tasks at home like cleaning, laundry, shopping, cooking and maintenance. But you can look at a range of other things, when you decide where to adjust:

- Responsibility for leisure time activities - childrens' and others'
- Responsibility for clothes and gear for children
- Responsibility for maintaining good relations with family and friends
- Responsibility for planning and organising holiday activities
- Your own leisure activities. Too few? Too many?
- Furnishing the house and allocation of space
- Sharing of maternity leave
- Time spent with children and partners
- Time spent with family and friends
- Time for yourself

In many ways thinking about the way you spend your time at home is difficult to separate from the thoughts you may have about content, purpose and consequently your satisfaction with your *working* life. For this reason it can be both necessary, but also very helpful, to include wishes and ideas from your working life in this phase of the negotiation of the balance at home. All the recent focus on work/life balance is good, but in order to restore balance, you need to think about and become aware of what you wish for both at home and at work, because you can then include even more elements in this negotiation with yourself. An example:

> A single mother with two teenage children senses, that she is badly needed at home just now. The children don't need her immediate care, as they did when younger but they have both expressed a need for her to be there: to talk to, to do shared activities with over and above just having dinner together. At the same time, this woman is very involved in her work where she is project manager on several big processes with a major client. This makes her reluctant to reduce her working hours to part-time, as she knows the project management will be transferred to someone else.

The challenge here is to map the needs and wants that make up the content of the negotiation this woman faces. If she decides to do something about spending more time with her children, she could think about the following questions:

> **How** do I want to spend more time with my children?
> **How** would a new division of my time look?
> **What** is it I want from the extra time spent with my children?
> **Which** part of my job is the most important to hang on to?
> **What** are the succes criteria for my contribution at work?
> **Which** possibilities do I have for living up to my own and others' expectations of me at work?

Most people spend time thinking about what they hope to achieve with their work and career. This doesn't mean that most of us have 5-year plans ready to present at any given time, but rather that we think about these things especially when confronted with what others do. This puts our own career in perspective and provokes thoughts about how we feel about our work. When our thoughts turn to challenges in our private life, we often feel stuck in the face of a range of seemingly insurmountable structures, demands and expectations we feel unable to do anything about. A classic example of this could be the perception that partners and children come before friends, when precious spare time is to be allocated. If this is a basic principle, then you may have already stumbled into the feeling that 'all time is spent' and that there are no more resources or time left over when the huge demand of partners, children and work have been satisfied. To find some time about which to negotiate can seem a challenge and completely unrealistic, but if this is the case, it's a sure sign that you need to negotiate something somewhere. Because you will become stressed out from always just being able to keep your head above water and manage to do just the most necessary things, especially if the framework you move within is too constricting. The very first negotiation you have with yourself, at home, by the kitchen table could have the following questions as a starting point:

> Do you spend your time and surplus energy the way you would like to?
> How will you get more time and surplus energy and what would you like to use it for?

As the day only has 24 hours this indicates that a negotiation is in place. That means that you won't get everything: You must find out what you most want, and then find out what you can live without. This is where you, again, may want to consider if things are as they should be. Then you can start dreaming about all the things you don't have but would like to have, and in this connection find out what the most important thing for you is. Prioritising is important especially, since you will need to involve others in your desire for the change that comes from your negotiation with yourself, and then it's vital to have thought about where to insist and where to give in. The dialogue in your mind might sound like this:

> **Your-sporty-you**
> "I wish I had more time for my favourite sport; rowing. It has previously been a huge part of my life and I miss it."

Your-rational-everyday-you
"That may be so, but rowing will cost both time and money, so that you can forget about"
Your-sporty-and-now-a-little-stubborn-you
"I have heard that song too many times. Something's got to happen. And I'll think about what it takes for me to be able to start rowing again."
Your-rational-and-rather-persistent-everyday-you
"If you absolutely insist, but then it will affect a lot of other things: your work, your family, your friends, your finances!"
Your-sporty-and-now-quite-determined-you
"If I look into the possibilities for starting to row again and what that demands and then consider how I spend both my working hours and my spare time, I wonder if I couldn't then organise to HAVE IT ALL?"
Your-rather-shaken-but-still-persistent-everyday-you:
"Okay, this is when you need to be realistic here. What would everyone else say? Isn't this more than just a little bit selfish?"
Your-very-motivated-sporty-you:
"I'll do it! I'll make a plan and talk to my family about it – the worst thing that can happen is that only parts of my plan succeed, but even that will be better than things are now!"

★ RECOMMENDED EXERCISES

Make time and space to get an overview of how you spend your time: how is the balance between your professional and private life? Is it as it should be or does it need adjusting? What activities or persons give you positive energy? Who or what drains your energy?

How would you like things to be? If you could have things exactly the way you wanted, how would your daily life be?

Prioritise things according to how important they are. Consider if some activities could be diminished in order to make room for something else? (For example, does one friendship need toning down in order to make space for another? Could driving the children to and from activities be shared? How clean does your home need to be, and who can help you?).

What would it take for you to make time for the things you appreciate that do not involve your nearest and dearest? Time for yourself?

PHASE 2: WHO NEEDS INFLUENCING?

Now comes the time to look into who will be affected by and therefore must be involved in this negotiation about the changes you want at home. What are their thoughts, and what wishes and wants might they put forward here? If what you have decided to change will have a serious impact on someone else's life and this makes you nervous that they will refuse, then there might be a strong urge also in this case to cut back on your demands. But here, at home, it is just as important as at work to look at what your first offer might be. To discover the nature of a good and ambitious first offer you need to know a lot about yourself, about the ones you need to negotiate with, and about the conditions you have for making this agreement. One way of reducing nervousness about asking for something you might get an initial 'no' to, is to look at the demand from various angles:

> Who is affected by your wish to change something?
> What consequences might this change have for them?
> What needs and wishes do they have?
> What are their thoughts on the thing you want?

The way to broach the subject could be that you actually just tell things the way they are; that you tell the other person what you want and why.

Here again it is important to follow up your wish with very few but good arguments, and then start investigating how this sounds to the other person. What wishes and wants do they have themselves? Here the interview technique is at play again, and the investigative journalist now needs to appear not just at work, but also at home. The whole purpose of this first part of the conversation is simply to get an even clearer overview of things. In the first phase, you found out what you wanted. Now the circle widens like rings in the water.

In an interview with the husband of a high profile Danish MP this man described how they have organised work at home. He is CEO of a large company, so with two busy schedules and small children, they have decided on some groundrules that suit them both: they never travel with work at the same time, so there will always be someone at home with the chilren at mealtime. They pick the children up from nusery themselves twice a week and weekends are sacred. As CEO he is continually trying to recruit more women for leadership positions, and he has noticed, that the question of how the balance between work and home would be affected by this acceleration of career *always* pops up in these potential new leaders' minds. He tries to provoke them by saying, that of course it is their choice but that perhaps their partners could change something to accomodate this career-move and make sure that the housework is divided equally? It may be that women generally don't think men know how to vacuum or wash the floor, but one place to start is to challenge them and find out!

Change takes time
To influence someone takes time. It means that the work you undertake in looking at all possibilities may become a steady undercurrent in your daily life. It may be, that this in the end gets you what you want. When change is needed and it involves others giving up on something it makes a difference how you introduce that change: whether you drop a bomb at dinner with your demands and force everyone to have an opinion about the matter right there and then. Or, if you introduce what you would like

to have or to change, ask what the others think about it just off the top of their heads and then leave things for a bit, letting everyone involved think about *what it will take* for them to agree to your proposal. By choosing the last approach you achieve more things at once. Firstly, you have announced that something will have to change or be improved, bringing something that is of importance to you out in the open. Secondly, you have acknowledged that others are affected by your wish for this change and thereby aim towards satisfying their interests as much as possible. This is done when everyone involved is starting to think about and get ideas on how to solve this. To focus on getting ideas and creating possible solutions is in itself a much more constructive way to work than a power struggle about who is right, which often leads to endless discussions and perhaps even fighting.

★ RECOMMENDED EXERCISES

When you have decided what new or different things you would like to achieve, then find out who will be affected by your wish for change. What will the consequences for them be? What are their wishes and wants?

Give time to those who will have to adjust in order to get used to the thought. Say what it is you want, and then ask what they think about this. What would it take for them to agree?

Spend some time alone as well as with the others involved getting ideas and producing possible solutions as to how everyone involved will get as much as possible out of this agreement to change or improve things. What do other couples do? Other families?

PHASE 3 – HOW WOULD YOU LIKE YOUR AGREEMENT TO LOOK?

Now it's almost time for making an actual agreement with those who have an interest in this negotiation. You have all aired your wishes and demands, your thoughts and interests and perhaps you have even inspired each other in the process. In other words, you have done what works best in any negotiation: to ask about and investigate your counterpart's needs and interests at the same time as telling them about yours.

Investigate wishes and interests
Let's go back to the case of taking up rowing again. This request has been on the table for a while now and in the interveening period the parties have had time to think. Now you are talking things through again, as the deadline for signing up for a new season of rowing approaches.

- "What do you think about my wish to start rowing again?"
- "I understand why you want to start again, but I'm worried what this will mean for the kids and me. I see before me a scenario where I'm left at home with the responsibility for bringing them and picking them up, and that you will be away from home much more."
- "I understand your worries as there will be quite a lot of things to coordinate. How will the scenario you describe affect your day?"
- "Well, it would put pressure on me at work knowing that I have to be back in time to pick up the kids and do the cooking. My work is so unpredictable, as you know."
- "My suggestion as to how we share the cooking is that we divide it equally. What would it take for you to be able to get back in time from work on the days you cook, no matter what?"
- "If I know it in advance, perhaps I can warn the others that I won't be available for meetings, and I might be able to do some work from home later in the evening."

- "Is there anything *you* would like to do more, now that we are talking about how we spend our time?"
- "Well actually yes, there is. I would like to start running on a more regular basis, and there are a couple of the guys from work who run together twice a week, but they start at 7 and that's right in the middle of our morning rush…"
- "Perhaps we can share the household duties in terms of days instead of being responsible for different tasks. How would you feel about that?"
- "Weeeeellll, that might just work. There are already days when one of us isn't here, and this also seems to work. But in this way we will end up never seeing each other as a family!"
- "You might be right there. So, apart from dividing up the days perhaps we could also reserve some evenings and mornings where we are all here? And I would actually also like for the two of us to spend some grown-up time alone together from time to time."
- "Let's hear what the kids say. If they have something they would like to contribute with?"

This conversation is influenced by your decision to really investigate and find out what the needs of your partner are, and what he thinks about your wish to change the routines in the family. It's a very good idea to make up your mind that you will ask about your partner's concerns and worries *before* you start making a lot of suggestions. When you ask, you'll get an answer, and some of these answers might sound provoking to you. But the more you work to get behind those wishes and demands and find out what underlying needs and interests they satisfy, the better prepared you will be for the next phase, which is all about getting ideas as to how all the involved parties will gain the most. You might want to do these 'interviews' or investigations bite-wise, and should you stumble on things that provoke either of you or make you angry, you can leave it for a bit, before you resume the investigation.

Many ideas for a solution
When those involved have aired their wishes and wants, you have looked at it all from various angles – then it will be time to think of good ideas that can accomodate everyone's wishes. This work demands a certain discipline as most people's impulse will be to focus immediately on the unreasonable in what the others are saying or very promptly suggest a solution. It is my strong recommendation that you structure the idea-making process and making this the next step of the negotiation following the investigative phase. It is always helpful to see things from many perspectives and angles, to turn everything upside-down and think of 'unrealistic' solutions and how they might work, and generally just spend some time producing ideas and suggestions:

> **What** would your day-to-day life look like if everyone got what they wanted?
> **What** effect would this have on everyone?
> **What** consequences would it have for their well being?
> **What** could you do to get to this state?
> **What** do others do?
> **How** is this dilemma solved in other environments? Other countries and cultures?
> **What** possibilities would arise, if the adults were to think up ideas that children normally do, and vice versa?

When you are talking about ideas for a possible agreement, it can be very tempting to say: "Well, this just isn't realistic. We can't do that!" But try not to. Stop whoever is thinking in terms of limitations (and a lot of us do!) and try as much as possible to brainstorm as many ideas as you can, so the negotiating table ends up groaning under the weight of a great many wishes, needs and, not least, possibilities and suggestions.

Construct an agreement
Now you'll be looking at a table full of all the wishes that the parties involved have presented as well as long lists of ideas to possible solu-

tions, and everyone has had time to think. Which means you have now reached the final stage of the negotiation: where the agreement must be made. This also means, that now is the time to strike deals. In order to do this, you must be prepared to give in on some of your demands, but also to keep working to achieve the fundamental wants and needs you have in this negotiation and not simply, or too quickly, give in.

This part of the negotiation is in fact something most of us are quite used to, as the 'quick deals' dominate most people's lives:

> **With your partner:**
> "Can you do the shopping on your way back, then I'll do the cooking?"
> "If I give you a lift to work, can I have the car today then?"
> **With your children:**
> "If you walk home with the others and I know where you are at all times, then it's ok to stay out 'till one AM"
> "If you really want to wear the ladybug shoes, then you must wear socks"
> "If you play on the computer now, then it's homework straight after supper"
> **With friends and family:**
> "If we're going to the cinema Friday at 5, can we have dinner together after the film?"
> "Can you pick up Gran on your way to the birthday party, then I'll find a present?"

Everyone can make agreements and deals, and many of these are made after a bit of back-and-forth, which is ... a negotiation. Here I must also say though, that there are, and always will and ought to be, things that are non-negotiable. Many have talked about the mistake of raising children so they won't do or accept anything without first negotiating it. In principle it's ok that they try, but the possibility of letting children negotiate something should be weighed against the very sensible recommendation that many experts put forward, that children need limits and clear rules to live by in many areas. This is why you also need to be able to say no to a negotiation, both for your own and for the other party's sake. In adult relationships there may also occur situations where one person feels that their boundaries have been disrespected, that they have felt themselves to be persuaded to do or accept things that are against their deepest values. Saying a clear 'no' can be difficult in the short run, but will be the much healthier option in the long run. Later on in this chapter we will look at a model for saying 'no' in a positive and constructive manner.

To have an eye for how often and how painlessly we make agreements with others in our day-to-day lives can be very useful when negotiating something with more far-reaching consequences. The experience you have as a master of the 'quick deal' can be directly translated to the bigger, and more serious negotiations, because these will also have the elements of 'trading something'. In these negotiations it is also, and absolutely, a good idea to make sure there is a balance in who gets or does what. Instead of forcing others to accept that things are changing around here, then you can spend some time trying to get those affected by the change on board. You can tell them why you think the change is a good idea, and listen to their reactions giving them an opportunity to share their feelings and thoughts about the issue, finding out what it will take for them to accept it. This will increase the likelihood that they will in fact honour the agreement, because if some kind of trade-off has taken place, then this means that everyone has gotten *something* out of the deal, and this principle, that we have looked at in previous chapters, also works in the negotiations you might have in your private life.

Back to your negotiations about the domestic duties and finding time and resources for you to start rowing again. Here are some of the possible 'deals' you could make:

- Making dinner could be shared with two days for each of you. As your rowing starts rather late, you can do the shopping for dinner on those days.
- Your partner takes the morning duty for two days and you have two days, so he gets time to run twice a week. This also means that you can get off to work earlier on those days and thus compensate for leaving earlier on the days you are on dinner-duty
- The children will start taking themselves off to training and they can bring home a friend for dinner max. twice a week if they like
- Friday morning everyone is at home and have breakfast together
- Every weekend the children get to decide on an activity
- You schedule in a 'grown-up day' once a month and take turns arranging it

Perhaps your wish to start rowing again and the ensuing talks and negotiations about this, has made not just your partner, but also your children, think about how they would like things to be at home, for themselves and with you. It may be that the 'deal' described above makes your days sound like strictly organised bootcamps, but see it more as an attempt to create a clear and fair (to the parties involved) distribution of duties at home, that will ultimately give everyone more freedom to do what they want instead of leaving it up to chance or 'who gets fed up with what first'. If there has not been any discussion about how everyone experiences the situation and how they would like things to be, then my guess is that negotiating the terms of living together will become something you do either non-verbally through demonstrating your dissatisfaction, or through spontaneous and perhaps not always particularly positive outbursts, when either one of you has had enough. Sharing household responsibilities is often highly affected by who is good at/most effective at cooking, cleaning, fixing the drains etc., or who is the first to buckle under to the sight of dirty clothes on the floor and unwashed dishes in the sink or the first to book a time for training/working late/going out with a friend.

Pia, an executive from a large bank with an impressive career behind her, in an interview I undertook with her, gave a great example of how you as a couple can agree on who gets to focus on their career when:

> 'I have great support at home, because I have a husband who has accepted that I have made a career for myself. But this is not something we have just done without talking about it, this is something we have discussed. We have been very conscious about the fact that, at certain times in our lives my possibilities and urge to further my career were greater than his. About a year after we have made a particular plan for this, we go away for a weekend alone and look at how things have worked out. Last time we went, we talked about my husband's career, and it turned out that he in fact would like a new job, which would make him less flexible than he is today. And so we have made arrangements, so this has become possible.'

This example illustrates how a general talk about what you want to do with your life can spark off new plans and consequently a need for revising the existing agreements you have. That a couple can negotiate their way to sharing the possibility for devoting oneself to making a career some time in one's life, will create a different kind of acceptance and patience, as both know that their turn will come. There may be many aspects and details of the agreements you make at home, because you might have a lot of wishes and wants you will need to accomodate. And you won't always succeed. But by negotiating your way to a balance at home, chances are that you'll end up with something positive as opposed to leaving things untill they become insufferable and you become angry, because making a change from that starting point will be much harder.

To be able to say no
If we stand back a bit and look at types of negotiations in our private life other than those between partners, then we'll find numerous examples:

> **With family and friends** we can negotiate about where and how to meet, hang out, remember each others' birthdays or celebrate special occasions
> **With friends** we also negotiate about spending time with or without our families and how this time should be spent
> **On boards in schools** or other institutions, sportsclubs or political groups we negotiate
> **Negotiations with neighbours** and in tenants- or homeowner associations
> **With other parents** about transportation of children, schooltrips and when they can have their first mobile

A tight daily schedule does not necessarily benefit from having more demands from people and projects outside the home squeezed in, especially if these demands are about one's time and attention. So here it is also very important to think about, on your own, what it is that you really want to spend your time doing; what will make the most sense to do; and how you can make things work best. This also applies to things you do more as a duty than because you really enjoy them. For example, certain family reunions or school activities for the children, work-related get-togethers or seeing people you no longer have much in common with, sometimes feel a lot like yet more duties to deal with. To *really* find out what you would like to do, how much (or little) spare energy you have and what you feel gives meaning to do for yourself and others, can help you in the situations where you have to say no to something you either haven't got time to do or just don't want to. It can be really difficult to say no, especially if you feel under pressure. In negotiation we always encounter a 'no' – as I've discussed earlier. If there was no 'no', then there wouldn't be a need to negotiate. So, you have to be prepared to get a no, when you ask for something. But what if you're not able to say no yourself to, for example, both supplying the food and having the whole, extended family over for Sunday lunch at your house on a regular basis? Or if you, yet again, are commended for your skills in taking minutes and organising all the paperwork for a meeting, and you end up having to do this every time your department has a meeting even though you would much rather not? Or the quiet acceptance of your neighbours use of the common areas in the building to store old furniture and other rubbish? If every time someone asks you to do something is a signal that now you can and may negotiate, then you need to be able to navigate and decide what you want to accept and what you clearly won't. When you get the feeling, that what you most of all want to do is say 'NO'- there are some classic reactions depending of course on the person or situation: You do, in fact, say 'NO' and perhaps you even fold your arms for emphasis. Or, you say yes even though you mean the opposite, or you don't say anything at all. In his book *The Power of a Positive No*, the negotiation expert William Ury looks into how you can both say no and find a solution to a problem. It all begins (again) with negotiating with yourself:

>   **What** lies behind your no to the proposal?
>   **When** you say no to this, what is it you in fact say YES to?
>   **What** wishes, needs and emotions in yourself do you respect by saying no?

So the first step is to find out, where your no comes from. When you discover the interests behind the no, then you may also find the strength you need to actually say it. If you have decided to spend less time on things like volunteering for events in your childrens' school in order to find the time to take dancing lessons with your partner, then your no to volunteering rests on a meaningful yes to something positive: sharing a positive experience with your partner. Ury's simple, but very effective model then looks like this:

>   **YES!**
>   - I want more quality time with my partner, and I want to learn how to dance

No
- This means I need to reduce the time I spend on other activities like, for example, volunteering at the school.

YES?
- Can we find other ways that I can support the school, that wouldn't demand the same amount of my time?

It is no coincidence, that Ury's model for 'a positive no' in effect becomes a negotiation, both with yourself and the world around you. William Ury is one of the authors of the bestselling book about constructive negotiation *Getting to Yes* which has been highly influential for more than 20 years.

★ RECOMMENDED EXERCISES

Our daily lives are full of negotiations. This means that we are all, in effect, experts at negotiating. Keep an eye on your negotiations and pay attention when what you do works. When you disagree with someone, suggest that you negotiate your way forward as an effective and more considerate way of resolving disagreement than arguments or fights.

Create the right framework for reaching an agreement. Make sure there is both time and space for the negotiation, and steer the process towards finding out what the parties want (interview) and coming up with ideas and suggestions for how to proceed (ideas)

Make agreements where all parties get maximum benefit from the agreement. Even if the negotiation is about something you want, then this could be your chance to also find out what the other person might want.

If it is difficult for you to say no, then find out what lies behind this feeling. Mostly you say no to one thing, because you want to do something else. What is that 'else'? Let the 'yes' to this be the support you need when saying no. Move on by looking into what other things you might be able to say yes to instead.

PHASE 4: THE AFTERMATH
– HOW DID WHAT YOU AGREED UPON WORK?

When you change something you need to get used to something new and different. This fact is almost always challenged by deeply anchored habits and notions about how things ought to be. The family that agreed on making space for both rowing and running and the children being more self-sufficient, might end up in a situation where broken bicycles and bad weather will make the children insist on being driven to and from activities. Perhaps the adults' work schedules all of a sudden demand many more hours in the workplace and all efforts to find the time to get to the rowing or do the cooking fall by the wayside. The daily running routine with a group of colleagues may never actually get going and thus the sense of balance will disappear. We all know what a precarious life our New Year's resolutions, or our decisions to eat healthy food and exercise, have. If you take the negotiation with yourself seriously, that is Phase 1 of the negotiation process, then you have a very good foundation for returning to what it was you really wanted, even if you do not succeed in getting it in the first place. If you have convinced yourself that the change you want is for the better, then it becomes much easier to persuade others.

Many possibilities
The point is that it is wise, at home as well as in the workplace, to follow up on the agreements you make. You can evaluate it after a time and in doing so discover and correct any imbalances that might have emerged, or even improve or expand upon the agreement you've made.

Perhaps talking about and actually making an agreement about certain things in your life together will make you want to confront any other imbalances there might be and take a close look at these to find out how things are and how you would like them to be. Here are some examples of negotiations in the private sphere:

> **A woman wanted to buy a flat in Berlin**, but was frustrated that her boyfriend was not particularly enthusiastic. When she sat down and thought about whose needs would be met in buying this flat (hers and not his) it opened up her mind to finding other ways of doing this together, where she was the main person responsible and he joined in according to need and interest.
>
> **For a number of years**, a younger man had suffered the consequences of a hereditary heart condition, which meant that he often would get quite seriously ill very suddenly but nevertheless refusing to see a doctor. His girlfriend was deeply worried about his health but he was very reluctant to go to the doctor for examinations because "they never find a solution anyway". After some time with these symptoms, the girlfriend negotiated her way to a deal that meant that next time he got ill, they would call out a doctor.
>
> **A married couple had to divide the space** available in the workshop they had built in their house. She would like to do her painting in there, listening to opera at a high volume, he would like a space where he could make his sculptures and do his home-improvement projects listening to smooth jazz. The solution became turning part of the garage into a workshop to fit the husband's needs exactly, and the wife got to keep the original space.
>
> **In a family they have organised the daily tasks** so that she often cooks and he does the dishes, by hand, that is. She does not interfere in how and when he does the dishes. Even if he waits until the last knife and fork have been used.

A father of four takes his children, one at a time, on weekend trips abroad. They get this trip as a 15-year birthday present, and the children decide entirely where they want to go. Other holidays and trips the parents decide on with the children, but these weekends are devoted to the child and what he or she wants.

A couple, each with a child from a previous relationship, spend Christmas apart. She takes her daughter to see her mother and he stays put and celebrates the holidays with his son. They all have a joint Christmas just before the official one.

★ RECOMMENDED EXERCISES

Follow up on the agreements you make. Look into whether and how they work for all parties.

If something is not ideal, keep doing the things that work, and make a new agreement about the rest. Negotiation takes place continually, and it is a very good tool for adjusting agreements.

Keep an eye out for other people's agreements and get inspired by those.

THE PARALLEL NEGOTIATION

In the negotiations that take place at home, there will also be this undercurrent that is the parallel negotiation. This is where you send signals to each other about sympathy and antipathy, respect and interest, acceptance or rejection. This is where your own boundaries are negotiated: What can you accept, and when have you had enough. Quite a large part of the private negotiations about actual tasks and responsibilities can end up in the 'invisible' parallel negotiation, if they are not dealt with openly.

Then the actual division of tasks and responsibilities becomes 'silent' in that you *demonstrate*, often physically, how much work you're actually doing, how tired you are and how unfair it all seems, instead of just bringing it up and talking about it. An undercurrent of blaming the other and overt dissatisfaction can develop, and this will soon be interpreted by the other person as lack of understanding and perhaps even disrespect.

In his book *Blink*, the author Malcolm Gladwell talks about a phenomenon he calls 'thin-slicing', which he describes as when our unconscious is "...sifting through the situation in front of us, throwing out all that is irrelevant while we zero in on what really matters...". It's a good image of what goes on in the parallel negotiation and Gladwell explores this in great and interesting detail in the book. One of the more unsettling examples he uses is the story of a psychologist John Gottman from University of Washington, who for many years has been working on designing a code-system to decipher the communication taking place between couples in minute detail. He has gotten so good at 'thin-slicing' the conversation between partners that after analyzing a one-hour conversation between the two, he can predict, with 95% accuracy, whether they will still be together 15 years down the track!:

> "He [Gottman]j has found that he can find out much of what he needs to know just by focusing on what he calls the Four Horsemen: defensiveness, stonewalling, criticism, and contempt. Even within the Four Horsemen, in fact, there is one emotion that he considers the most important of all: contempt. If Gottman observes one or both partners in a marriage showing contempt toward the other, he considers it the single most important sign that the marriage is in trouble" (*Blink;* Malcolm Gladwell)

As in the parallel negotiation at work, it is all about being aware of how you want other people to percieve you. Are your partner and family members really happy about the fact that you take on far too much at home and as a consequence often get tired and grumpy? A single dad once told me, how one night, when doing the dishes, he was hit by the question as to whether he was using his time in the best way: standing alone in the kitchen doing the dishes, or lying on the floor playing with his young son the last hour before he was due to go to bed? Choosing, as he did, to let dishes be dishes and spend time with his child will no doubt benefit their relationship and thereby make other, small and large, negotiations the two of them will have much easier. The parallel negotiation of our relationships is a huge part of our private lives as well, and here also we have the possibility to influence 'the story of me'. As at work, I don't think a lot of people prefer spending their lives with a martyr, who will always put others' needs before their own and thereby become both bitter and resentful. To draw attention to the fact that there are things you would like to change sends a signal, in the parallel negotiation, that you trust the person you're with, that you would like to work on your relationship, and that you respect yourself and your own needs enough to listen to them. In Appendix VII we look at the roles you either get lumped with or take on willingly, both at work and at home, and what the effect of these choices are.

// RESEARCH ON...
HEROES OR VILLAINS, OR 'WHO'S RIGHT'?

Most people have a fundamentally positive story about themselves, and this is no coincidence. Firstly we all have 'private data' (experiences and impressions) and consequently a storyline we live our life by ('I'm a good mother, a helpful friend, a competent boss'). That we are deeply embedded in our own experiences and impressions is what researchers sometimes call 'the egocentric bias'. This bias can lead to heated discussions, for example in relationships, where both parties claim that they do 80% of the housework and only instigate 20% of the arguments surrounding them. Secondly, we have a need and an interest in constructing stories about ourselves that underpin our identities as responsible, caring, competent and good people. Problems arise when we in this manner have delegated the role of hero to ourselves, which leaves only the role of being the 'villain' or 'the problem' for the other person. That we appoint this unflattering role to the other person as someone who is, for example, patronising, inconsiderate, incompetent or downright unpleasant will again lead to us noticing and digging out evidence to support this perception. This phenomena is called 'stereotypical bias' and can result in a conflict escalating. It can be very difficult to change this often quite stubborn perception, that it is the other person who is to blame for all the problems you face. This illustrates again how vital it is, that when you encounter disagreement, spend some time trying to find out how things are perceived on the opposite side of the table. If we are as 'biased' as this research indicates, then it makes very little sense spending time and energy finding out who is right. It is far more interesting finding out *how* you move on from here *in spite* of the differences in world views.

(Sheila Heen and Douglas Stone; *Perceptions and Stories*)

That we attribute the people with whom we make deals certain roles can greatly influence our negotiations. Perhaps you have given yourself the role of the person who needs to be responsible for your home in an overall sense, as this demands a talent for organisation and overview, and you don't think the other person has these talents. This role can quickly become self-fulfilling, as the other person now has to fight to get this 'job' and then prove that they can fill the post. If this role isn't the most attractive one to begin with, then it will come as no surprise that most people would happily give it up. In the same manner it can be dangerous to categorise another person as 'selfish', 'forgetful' or 'irresponsible', because you will tend to look for things that confirm your analysis of the other and thereby fuel this tendency in them. Psychologist Gitte Haslebo recounted to me that on a course she runs, she sometimes does an exercise with participants, where a group of 6-8 people are asked to discuss a subject. Before they start, each has a label glued to their foreheads with a particular characteristic written on it, which they don't see themselves. A characteristic could be 'argumentative', 'collaborative', 'creative' or 'negative'. As the discussion unfolds, the participants slowly begin behaving more and more like the label they have been given! So, it seems that we are all in danger of treating people according to the 'labels' we create for them ourselves or those others have given to them. ("Don't bother asking her to be group leader, because she is a total scatterbrain"), and it's contagious! There are also many experiments made with schoolchildren, where you *randomly* separate children into two groups and label one 'the clever team' and the other 'the unintelligent team'. The teachers that got these groups were told that their groups were divided according to ability, and thus didn't know that the children were randomly assigned to the groups. After a relatively short time it became very obvious, that 'the clever team' did far better than 'the unintelligent team' – simply because of the way the teachers had perceived these children and adjusted their teaching accordingly. Children who are constantly described as forgetful have a very good explanation for themselves why they can't remember to put their clothes away or tidy up the dishes after themselves *every* time. That this characteristic is far less prevalent when it's all about remembering codes for a computer game or when and where to meet up with their friends, just makes you wonder. Keep an eye out for whether you give people in your surroundings roles or characteristics that might not do them, nor you, any good. As I mentioned earlier, I firmly believe that we all have the possibility to behave differently from situation to situation, from one relationship to another. To be aware of, and trying to avoid getting stuck with negative views of the people around you will also give them the opportunity to do something different, or better. This openness is particularly helpful when you negotiate, if you keep focusing on the subject matter (we need to do the food shopping for the whole week in one go) and not on a – negative – judgment of the person you negotiate with (he has neither the know-how nor the overview to do the shopping *right*).

Emotions in negotiations

It is hard to avoid emotions in negotiations, because it will always be *about* something that matters, to a greater or lesser degree. Most negotiations are full of a range of emotions that will affect the negotiators before, during and even after the process is over. Some negotiation experts have recently begun taking an interest in these emotions and have looked at to what use they might be put. Traditionally negotiation training has been all about how to isolate or eliminate emotions, so they wouldn't disturb the process.

In their book *Beyond Reason*, writers Daniel Shapiro and Roger Fisher introduce a way to look at feelings as both 'lens' and 'lever'. Emotions can become the lens through which you view your counterpart, which can help enhance one's own understanding of how they react and behave. For example, some of what you ask the other person in a negotiation might produce a sharp reaction, perhaps even an angry response. Instead of being offended by this and rolling up your sleeves to give as good as you get, you might also choose to examine what lies behind this reaction. In this way the strong emotions displayed become an indication of what the other person finds important. The authors have identified five basic needs that, if not met, could result in negative reactions. These five needs would be:

> **Appreciation** – of a person's thoughts, feelings, actions
> **Association** – to be a part of a community and recognised as such
> **Autonomy** – the wish to be able to decide for yourself on important issues in life
> **Status** – to have and be fully recognised for the status you have
> **Role** – to be given the roles that make sense to you

The theory is that you can make sure to meet all these needs or as many as possible, when you negotiate with others. If you get resistance or an angry or wounded reaction from the other person, you can use these pointers to try and find out where the reaction comes from. To ignore these basic needs and thereby create a kind of deficit could sound like this, if we look at the negotiation from earlier on in this chapter:

- "I would like to get the time and opportunity to start rowing again"
- "I don't think you quite mean that, if you stop and think. Where on Earth would you find the time? And what about the kids and their needs? I really don't see any point in having this conversation, it's out of the question"
- "That's just too much! Why do you get to decide this? What about all the things you take time out to do? It's just not fair!"
- "But...I thought we were agreed on this. We have talked about it before, you know?"

It is possible that this subject has been discussed before so the very emotional response might not be so surprising. But the response to the request violates all the basic needs of his partner, so the negotiation is derailed immediately and moves on to be about a lot of other, and much more difficult, stuff: their relationship, respecting each other, the possibility of deciding to do something for oneself, the role and status she has in the family.

Firstly, a strong response gives a clear picture that here is something that has a really powerful meaning for one of them. It is obviously very important for her to do this. This will give her partner an indication that perhaps this is not a request that can just be brushed off. Secondly, the response gives hints as to what it will take for her to be happy – *if* he takes the time and makes the effort to investigate and find out what interests lie behind her strong wish to start rowing again.

It is not the intention that we should all become amateur psychologists for each other as soon as we meet an emotional response and start asking questions about the other person's childhood and relationship with her mother, in order to find out what the problem is. This model is in tune with my general and often repeated recommendation: Start by looking into what the parties want and the interests behind these demands. It's relevant at the workplace but certainly also in the negotiations at home. Here it is vital to find out, if the five basic needs are met in both parties, or how you work your way towards a balance here as well. The fear of provoking strong feelings in another person can perhaps be lessened by having these tools to work with when they do arise; the lens as a picture of how we need to look at and investigate the picture created by the emotions, and the lever as the tool to help us move forward by trying to restore a balance.

Negotiating your own limits
In close relationships you are constantly challenged and pushed with regards to your own personal limits. When you live and work with other people, then you cannot avoid having to compromise. You can give in to other people's demands and wishes, sacrifice yourself and live with a burning sense of injustice and anger as the general timbre of your life. But you can also negotiate your relationship with others in a way that protects your own limits and thereby look after yourself. The first step to acting in the parallel negotiation, both at work and at home, is when you really look inside and discover when something or someone is too much, too unfair or simply wrong in your moral and ethical eyes and deciding to change this.

✶ RECOMMENDED EXERCISES

Have a look at your relationships and try to discover, when you are busy 'parallel negotiating'. What lies just below the surface? What signals are you receiving and how are they affecting your relationship?

Strong feelings are often an indication, that you're dealing with something that is important to a person. To recognise each others' strong emotions and look into what they are a sign of, can make everyone wiser.

If there are things or relationships you consider 'unfair' – see this as the starting point of a negotiation and not a fight.

CHAPTER 6

NEGOTIATORS OF THE FUTURE

NEGOTIATORS OF THE FUTURE

As men and women, siblings and parents, we all have a big responsibility for how future generations will be able to negotiate good and balanced agreements in spite of the range of filtres such as gender, age or ethnicity that abound. The possibilities are present to change and adjust at home and at work and to change these frames if need be, but it demands attention, taking an active stand and... negotiating.

Of equal worth
In her book *Of Equal Worth – the way to bring up happy boys and girls with healthy self-esteem*, author Nina Frank's clear message is that we as adults need to be the right examples to children. We need to be role models that clearly show that there is absolutely no reason to let your gender stand in your way. It starts at home, in nursery and at school, where circumstances to an alarming degree make boys and girls behave gender-stereotypically. If you, as Nina Frank and I do, refuse to believe that girls' and boys' brains are so very different as to qualify women to certain things and men to others, then it's time to roll up your sleeves and start changing the traditional perception of gender. In her book, Nina Frank has a telling example of how this work could be done (my translation):

> "...Women are brought up to think that it is more important not to be excluded from the group than to look after your own needs. This has a lot of consequences. One of them being that there are so few women in executive positions in society. The women who'll say: "I'm having the last biscuit on the plate" or "It's time for an increase in my salary", are few and far between. I was coaching a mother, who had big problems in this front. I asked her, what it would take for her to go home and literally take the last biscuit from the plate. She felt awful just thinking about it. Then I asked her, how she was going to teach her children, to 'take biscuits' in their lives. This made her do it. For their sake. If

it feels utterly wrong, then at least we can do it for the childrens' sake. Because children will do what we do, not what we tell them to do. They look at us and then they do, what we do. One of the most important things you can do in your relationship is to help each other fulfill our needs. To say to each other: "Isn't it about time you went to the cinema?"

Change through negotiation
In an article in the Negotiation Journal, the two authors Hannah Riley Bowles and Kathleen L. McGinn investigate how negotiations at the workplace and at home are heavily interlinked[vol. 24., November 2008]. They conclude that when tasks and responsibilities at home are negotiated, then the person making the most money gets away with taking on less. At the same time, these negotiations are coloured by attitudes as to how the different genders normally behave, for instance attitudes to what it means to be a good mother. These two aspects play a role in creating an imbalance in both the negotiations about housework and also to the negotiations at work, where women more often than men try to accomodate the domestic chores into their worklife, resulting in spending less time at work and opting for more flexibility rather than higher wages etc. This affects their actual salary negatively, which again means, that they take on more of the domestic chores because they make less than their partners. Their recommendations for correcting this imbalance is also a summary of much of the advice in this book:

> **Discover unfounded limitations**
> When we negotiate, we are often hampered by an inability to see how we can move forward if two things are not immediately reconcilable. It becomes impossible to figure out how to combine a high-level management position with being the mother and/or the partner you think you ought to be. The moment that you as a negotiator start getting more ideas and alternatives on the table to think beyond the traditional solutions, and especially if you involve those affected by the negotiation in finding those alterna-

tives, then you are on the road to expanding the field and opening up new paths to follow. You move away from 'either-or' towards 'both-and'.

Get more and better information
When women tend to operate more in all women networks, especially at work, then they don't get as varied and nuanced information as in mixed groups about, for example, how much other people in the organisation earn. When you want to find out your worth, to benchmark, then it's well worth your while to look far and wide and spend time seriously investigating what others earn, particularly those you strive to be like. This will help you 'upping' your demand to an ambitious level.

Become aware of gender as a filtre
When you discover that you are treated in a gender stereotypical way, the first step is to do something to avoid this having negative consequences. To speak openly about sharing household tasks with those you live with can reveal whether an imbalance in the sharing of the housework has something to do with traditional perceptions of who does what in the home. From here it becomes easier to renegotiate a fairer deal.

Choose partner with care
When you choose where to work, most people look at criteria such as; exciting tasks, good salary, inspiring colleagues etc. One important criteria could also be to look into whether this is a company with a culture where you openly discuss and negotiate your way to solutions that fit the individual. Is there a genuine interest in both management and employees being satisfied? Is there room for creative and unorthodox solutions to problems? A prerequisite for being able to negotiate your way to better conditions at work and at home, thus making sure not to sacrifice your career because of an impossible work-life balance, is that the people you negoti-

ate with *actually* think that a win-win solution is best. This goes for partners both at home and at work.

There are many situations in which unfavourable conditions prevent people from getting what they want. Once you discover what holds you back, then you also have the opportunity to try and change this. To change things can create resistance and scepticism in your surroundings, which is why it can be tempting to let sleeping dogs lie and hope that things will work out automatically. This is just not always good enough, and at the end of the day it is our own responsibility to try and change what we're not happy with. If we don't want to achieve this change by twisting peoples' arms, forcing them to give in, then negotiation is a possibility. We have to make it very clear how our surroundings will benefit from relinquishing something or changing their ways. But when they realise that by doing so they get happy employees, partners, wives, husbands and children – then perhaps this happiness will actually bounce right back.

Go on, have that last biscuit and enjoy it!

APPENDIX I:
EXPLORING YOUR OWN NEGOTIATIONS

Step 1: You have taken part in many negotiations having reached agreements with someone when the result was not a given. This means that you have negotiated many things , both at home and at work. Think about the last couple of weeks and write down what you have negotiated with others, and what you gained from these negotiations. One way of thinking about this is discovering instances where you have had an opinion about something that is different from the other person's opinion. This will no doubt have led to negotiations at one point or another.

Who?	Who initiated the negotiation?	What did you negotiate about?	What was the result?
Your boss			
Your colleagues			
Collaborators			
Clients/customers			
Familymembers			
Partner			
Children			
Friends			
Others			

Step 2: What are your thoughts on:
- Who initiated the negotiation?
- The extent of the result you reached?
- Possible negotiations you might initiate with one or more of the parties mentioned above?

APPENDIX II: ANALYSING A GOOD PROCESS

Think of a really good negotiation you have participated in. It might have been a great deal you made with someone at work, or perhaps it was something you agreed on with a member of your family.

Was there something about the way you prepared yourself that worked well?

What did you do to make sure it became a good negotiation? Which of the negotiation tools did you use?
- Listening and showing an interest in your counterpart
- Respecting and accepting that others have different viewpoints
- Building strong relationships and caring about them
- Being creative and innovative when looking for possible solutions
- Being able to focus on reaching an agreement rather than winning the argument
- Being true to your own goals yet flexible in reaching them?

What did your counterpart do?

Was there something in the circumtances that made this a good process?

What process-tools were used in a constructive way?:
- The physical framework?
- The way you communicated?
- How participants were involved?
- Keeping an overview of things?
- Timeframe?
- The way you worked on content?
- The facilitation of the meeting/conversation?

What made you able to land the deal?
What has happened since then?
What is the most important thing you have learned from this negotiation?

APPENDIX III:
GENDER AS FILTER

Step 1: Think about situations in which you have become aware of your gender:
- What made you aware of it here?
- How did it manifest?
- Who instigated the situation?
- What did you do?
- How did you feel about being made aware of your gender?
- Did it affect your possibilities for action?
- How and to what degree?

Step 2: Consider:
- Is there something about the terms under which you work or negotiate relating to gender that you would like to change?
- Could you negotiate about it? Openly or indirectly?
- What ways of communicating or acting can position you differently? And could this help strengthen your position and power?
- Who could you use as a rolemodel here?
- What does she or he do in the parallel negotiation to make them powerful?
- In what networks and social spheres can you strengthen the parallel negotiation about you?

APPENDIX IV:
EXPANDING YOUR LIMITS FOR WHAT YOU CAN ASK FOR

Step 1: In what areas do you wish to develop or change at work?
- Areas of responsibility?
- Tasks?
- Actual responsibilities?
- Influencing content?
- Collaborating with colleagues?
- Collaborating with superiors?
- Collaborating with customers/clients?
- Physical work environment?
- Disposal of your time?
- Feedback and recognition?
- Respect?
- Pay and general working conditions?

Step 2: What would you like these improvements to consist of?
Actual and concretely? Do not let yourself be limited to one thing only, think broadly and ambitiously:
- What would you like?
- What would make you really happy?
- What do you hope for in your wildest dreams?

Step 3: Place all your wishes in a circle according to how easy/difficult it would be for you to ask for. The closer to you, the easier.

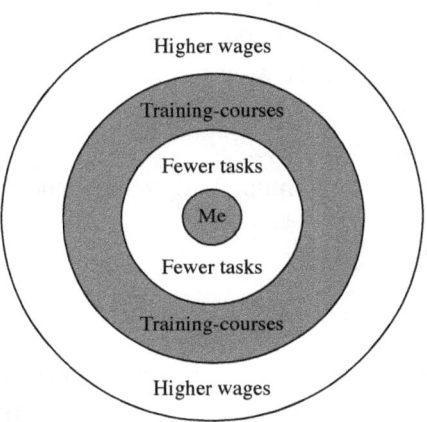

Step 4: Think of a situation where you felt out of your depth but actually made it anyway. What did you do? Why did you succeed? What did you learn from this experience? Use this experience when you embark on step 5

Step 5: Start by asking for what you find the easiest (that which is closest to you in the circle) and work your way out.
The circle can be made wider as you go along as you gradually expand your limits for what you feel okay about asking for

APPENDIX V:
THE AMBITIOUS FIRST DEMAND

Step 1: Think about what you want; what will make you really happy with the negotiation? (the ambitious offer)
Write down what you actually want to say when you present your demands/wishes:
- "I would like to have…"
- "Because…" (maximum 3 arguments, and they have to be good ones)
- "What do you think?"

Step 2: Find a helper, who can act as your counterpart and brief this person about the situation and who you will meet in the negotiation and their likely reaction. Present your demands/wishes and let your helper act your counterpart in as authentic a way as possible. Your helper will also make notes of what you are saying.

Step 3: Swap roles. Your helper gets your notes and with those and their own notes from the first round, you go through the negotiation again with you as the counterpart and the helper repeating what you said in round 1. Look out for what works and where you might want to adjust.

Step 4: Talk to your helper about what went well.

APPENDIX VI:
WORK-LIFE BALANCE

Step 1: Look back over the past 6 months and think about how you divide your time between the following areas:
- Work (also the work you do from home)
- Domestic chores
- Leisure activities with family and friends
- Time for yourself

Step 2: Draw a circle and distribute time in chunks according to how you spend it.

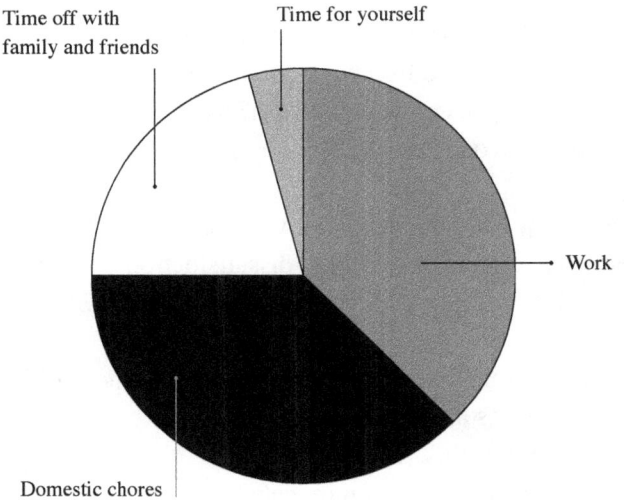

Step 3: Draw another circle and distribute time as you wish you could do it

Step 4: What negotiations would it take with yourself and your surroundings to achieve this balance? (You can use the model from Appendix IV to work out what you want)

APPENDIX VII:
YOUR ROLES AT WORK AND AT HOME

Step 1: What roles do you have at work? (For example; colleague, organisor, partyplanner, friend, timekeeper, tidy-up person, comforter, spokeswoman etc.) Make a list and consider involving others to discover what your roles really are.

Step 2: What roles do you have at home? (For example; friend, food-provider, homework-assistant, sheriff, mistress etc.) Make a list and consider involving others in discovering them all.

Step 3:
What roles on the two lists have you taken on yourself? Mark with √
What roles on the two lists have others given you? Mark with **X**
What roles are you comfortable with? Mark with ☺
What roles are you tired of? Mark with ☹

Step 4: What are your immediate thoughts about this picture?
Is there a pattern? (For example, dissatisfaction with the roles others give you?)

Can you adjust the roles and increase focus on the positive ones and minimize the less attractive ones?
What can support this change:
- ➤ The way you communicate?
- ➤ The way you behave?
- ➤ The jobs you take on?
- ➤ The limits you set?
- ➤ What you allow yourself to do? Or not to do?

RECOMMENDED LITERATURE

The Negotiator's Fieldbook – Andrea Kupfer Schneider, Christopher Honeyman editors American Bar Association 2006

Getting to Yes – Roger Fisher and William Ury
Random House Business 2003

Getting Past No – William Ury
Random House Business 1992

Beyond Reason – using emotions as you negotiate Roger Fisher and Daniel Shapiro Random House 2006

The Power of a Positive No – William Ury
Mobius 2008

Everyday Negotiation – Deborah Kolb
Jossey-Bass 2003

Women Don't Ask – Linda Babcock and Sara Laschever
Princeton University Press 2003

Ask For It – Linda Babcock and Sara Laschever
Piatkus Books 2008

The Myth of Mars and Venus – Deborah Cameron
Oxford University Press 2007

Language and Gender – Penelope Eckert, Sally McConnell-Ginet
Cambridge University Press 2003

Off-ramps and On-ramps – Sylvia Ann Hewlett
Harvard Business School Press 2007

Her Place at the Table – Deborah Kolb
Jossey-Bass 2004

Madam Secretary – Madeleine Albright
Pan Books 2004

ABOUT THE AUTHOR:

Malene Rix, born 1965, is an executive advisor and trainer in negotiation, process-facilitation and leadership working with a range of private- and public sector clients.

Read more on: www.malenerix.dk

www.ingramcontent.com/pod-product-compliance
Lightning Source LLC
Chambersburg PA
CBHW070542090426
42735CB00013B/3055